The Art of Body Piercing

Everything You Need to Know Before,
During, and After Getting Pierced

GENIA GAFFANEY

iUniverse, Inc.
Bloomington

The Art of Body Piercing
Everything You Need to Know Before,
During, and After Getting Pierced

iUniverse books may be ordered through booksellers or by contacting:

iUniverse
1663 Liberty Drive
Bloomington, IN 47403
www.iuniverse.com
1-800-Authors (1-800-288-4677)

Because of the dynamic nature of the Internet, any web addresses or links contained in this book may
have changed since publication and may no longer be valid. The views expressed in this work are
solely those of the author and do not necessarily reflect the views of the publisher, and the publisher
hereby disclaims any responsibility for them.

Any people depicted in stock imagery provided by Thinkstock are models,
and such images are being used for illustrative purposes only.

Certain stock imagery © Thinkstock.

ISBN: 978-0-5954-8275-7 (sc)
ISBN: 978-1-4759-5485-2 (hc)
ISBN: 978-0-5956-0361-9 (e)

Printed in the United States of America

iUniverse rev. date: 12/28/2012

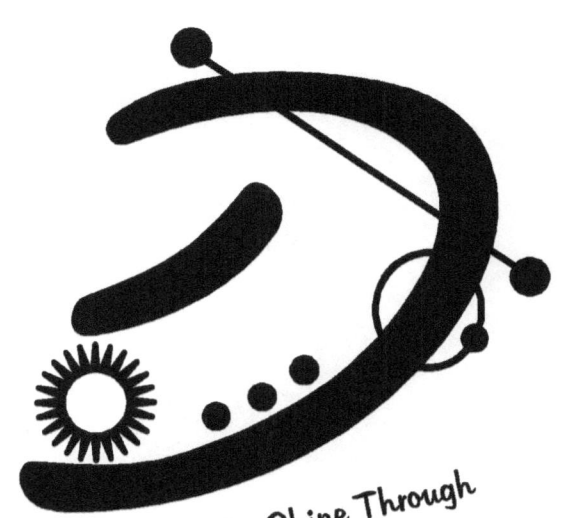

Let the Light Shine Through

This book is dedicated to my husband, Chad, who never imagined he would be married to a body piercer. Thank you for your love and support and for always encouraging me to make my dreams come true.

This book is also dedicated to my loving parents, who taught me to reach for the stars.

Contents

Introduction

B ody piercing has become commonplace in our society. You see it everywhere, from the waitress in a restaurant to the businessman walking down the street. People usually love it or hate it. Those who love it *really* love it, and those who hate it, well, we've all encountered them. Everyone has an opinion about it. One thing is for sure, people love talking about their piercings and planning their next one. It's fun to accessorize our bodies, isn't it? It's a very personal thing: we take our piercings with us everywhere, and we love to show them off.

This book will be helpful for anyone who wants to learn more about body piercing. It is written to a general audience, but it will be helpful to anyone with an interest in body piercing on a personal level. And for the person who is already piercing and wants to learn more about the craft, or for business owners who are already selling body jewelry but want to learn more about it, this book will give more information than has ever been written in a book about body piercing. It does not contain information on how to perform the actual piercings, as this is something that should be taught in person by a trained professional. There is a lot to learn about body piercing: jewelry, tools, aftercare, what to do about infection, and the piercing process itself. There is more to piercing than shoving a needle through the skin. It is important to know the gauges of the jewelry and to understand which length or diameter works best for which piercing and why.

I believe in being in the right place at the right time—and recognizing that you are in the right place at the right time. This is what led me to become a body piercer. I hope you enjoy your journey through my book. Just like you, I love body piercing. It is my career, my life. Although I love body piercings, I am not fanatical about it, and to look at me you would never guess what I do.

I am fortunate to own my own body-piercing business. From the beginning, I realized that I have the responsibility to educate the general public about piercing, and that is what I have done. It's important to provide correct information about piercing, because there is too much incorrect information floating around. If you read testimonials about my stores, the one comment that surfaces over and over about my staff is how knowledgeable they are and how ready they are to answer any question.

Everyone has their own boundaries about what is right for their body. I am not trying to borrow from other cultures. I respect the history of body piercing, and I am fascinated with piercings from other cultures. The piercing I do is artistic and expressive, but it's also quite simply a matter of accessorizing the body. Our bodies have become the canvas on which to create art.

I don't look like a body piercer, and I've always believed this is one of the things that helped make me successful. I used to be a paralegal for a law firm in San Diego. My hobby was making and selling jewelry. Through a very lucky chain of events, in 1993 I got out of the paralegal field, moved back to north Idaho (where I grew up), and bought a small jewelry store where I sold sterling silver jewelry at our local mall. Three years later, I bought my second store in Spokane, Washington. I was thirty-six years old when I became a body piercer, and I cannot imagine being in any other profession.

It was a couple of years before I started selling body jewelry. I began hesitantly, not really understanding gauges and diameters, but learning as much as I could. The company that provided me with body jewelry during that time was incredibly helpful. During the mid-1990s, body piercing still had not hit the mainstream, and there were very few vendors selling body jewelry. I started out with what was safe, selling navel jewelry, and slowly incorporated jewelry for other piercings into my inventory. It was fun, and my customers were very excited to see body jewelry in the mall. I wanted to have my own belly button pierced, but I was nervous about entering a tattoo shop and that was the only place doing body piercing at that time.

I remember the first time I hired a girl who had her belly button pierced. It made her seem very exotic. At that time body piercing wasn't really discussed in the community where I lived. In my store, we pierced ears with piercing guns and changed earrings for our customers. I thought about performing body piercing—I even talked about it a little bit. Then I was offered an opportunity to learn the art of body piercing. Talk about being in the right place at the right time! I didn't hesitate; I just did it and I never looked back.

That day changed my life forever. I have to say that I was a bit nervous to tell my parents my exciting plans to become a body piercer. They were in their seventies at the time, so obviously body piercing wasn't something that they really thought about. They were out of town when I told them. Neither one reacted to the news; in fact, they didn't say anything! When they returned home from their trip a couple of months later, they came to my store in Spokane to see what it was all about. They have turned out to be my biggest fans. I have brought my mom to work with me, and she sits and watches me pierce and talks to my customers.

My dad always told me to find something to do that I loved, because if I loved doing it, it wouldn't feel like work—and that was important because I was going to be doing it for a long time. Little did I know I would love body piercing. Aside from being a body piercer, I love owning my own business. My parents can come to see me at my store, and I started bringing my daughter to work with me when she was almost three. She was raised at my stores, The Sterling Stop in Coeur d'Alene, Idaho, and Silver Safari in Spokane, Washington, both of which are in shopping malls. Three of the girls who work for me also bring their kids to work. Owning your own business, no matter what it is, gives you this freedom, which I feel is important and lacking in our society. Our children should see what we do and know where we work. Anyone who is self-employed should take advantage of this wonderful opportunity.

The woman who trained me to pierce came to my store to do my training, which is incredibly rare (she did not live in my town), and I was fortunate to learn to pierce on my own customers. It is highly important to be trained by the right person. You need to connect with this person, and you need to feel comfortable with him or her. I had spoken to her on the phone a few times, and I was as nervous as I was excited to meet her. I had only seen the body piercers in local tattoo shops who were mostly men and looked very intimidating. This woman showed up at my store and looked like someone's mom! She was in her forties, and the only piercings she had were a tragus and a conch piercing. I was trained to do freehand piercing, and at the time, I didn't know there was any other way to pierce. I've never pierced with clamps, and I cringe anytime I see them used. She trained me to pierce the navel, nose, eyebrow, nipple, earlobe, and cartilage. I created my own set of care instructions for each piercing, which explained in detail how to care for a new piercing. I have never seen a piercing studio give care instructions as complete as mine; most studios do not give written care instructions at all. Later, I was able to teach myself to pierce the daith, rook, industrial, and anti-tragus (ear piercings—see photos and glossary).

Several months later, I flew in another piercer (who had been trained by the same piercer as the woman who trained me) to my store to train me on tongue and labret (lip) piercings. He taught me how to pierce using a clamp. I did not like the clamp method for the obvious reason that if you squeeze too hard on the tool, the handles on the clamp will lock while attached to the customer's tongue or lip, which can cause extra swelling, discomfort, and bruising. Through one of my suppliers, I learned about a tool called a Tuttle Tweezer, which has the same purpose as a clamp but does not have a locking handle. I can control the amount of pressure I put on a tongue or lip, without the risk of locking the tool on my customer, causing him or her further discomfort.

I did not connect with this second piercer as I did with the female piercer. Even though he was very nice, he was not as professional as I expected him to be. The written care instructions he gave me to use were not completely accurate and had inappropriate information on them. Once again, I created my own set of care instructions for lip and tongue piercings and added good aftercare tips. This was my first hands-on experience learning that just because someone is a body piercer does not mean he or she is doing everything correctly. This reinforces the importance of being trained by the right person. If a piercer is trained by someone who does not have a complete understanding of piercing and aftercare, he or she will learn the same incorrect methods and continue a cycle of bad piercers.

I am a certified body piercer. I was required to perform four hundred body piercings in order to receive my certification. I have performed over seven thousand piercings and overseen thousands more in my stores. After I was certified, I did considerable research in the library, in bookstores, and on the Internet to learn more about my new career. What I found was that information on this subject was nearly nonexistent. There were no books on body piercing. The little bit of information I was able to find was sketchy at best and was not completely accurate. The only book I could find centered on tattoos and only had a small chapter about body piercing. Unfortunately, some of the information about piercing in that book was not correct.

When I decided to start writing this book, I went back on the Internet to see what I could find on the subject of body piercing. I wanted to know if anyone was distributing a book or had a website with accurate information. I was looking to find good information about what to do with infected piercings and what is being suggested today for aftercare. I found that after several years, one thing has not changed: there is still very little information on body piercing that is accurate or available. Most of the information distributed on the Internet is wrong. The majority of websites on body piercing are putting out information not written by body piercers. Most of these websites contain articles written by everyday people simply offering their opinion on the subject. It is not factual or written based on experience working in the body-piercing field. This frustrates me. The public looks to the Internet for information from body piercers, and it bothers me that many piercers also post information that is not always correct.

Body piercers all have an opinion on what is right and wrong when it comes to piercing. Body piercers do not always agree with each other and, in many cases, they do not use the same techniques. In my experience, I have seen many piercers who do not have the skill needed to become a great piercer. This may be because of limited knowledge on the part of the piercers training them or the lack of research on their own to learn everything they can about the field they work in.

All of the information written in this book is backed by years of experience, research, and trial and error, piercing thousands of customers, and learning what works and what does not. In my stores, we have done over eighty-six thousand body and ear piercings in our first twelve years. I have tested different types of body jewelry, care solutions, and tools in order to find what I believe to be the best.

When you are working with the human body, every piercing is different. One person's body may not necessarily react the same to a piercing as another's would. And what is unusual and unexplained about the human body is that for one person, every piercing experience that person has can be different. For example, what worked on someone's ear piercing—jewelry, care, etc.—may not work on that same person's navel piercing. Some people can wear surgical steel in their ears, but their belly button will not accept it so they have to wear titanium or gold. The human body is very mysterious, and it is the job of the body piercer to learn about how the body reacts to certain metals.

Being a body piercer is one of the greatest jobs out there. Every day is interesting. Every day you come home with a new and very amusing story about someone you pierced. You meet great people. When my body piercers get together, there are endless stories told about their jobs, customers, and piercings. When you pierce people, you are giving them something they want, something that makes them happy. It is very rewarding.

This is not a job for the faint of heart, and it takes, in my opinion, a very special person to do this job well. Occasionally someone will ask us why piercing is so expensive. The answer is that the customer is paying for expertise. I am proud to say that I have always taken a different approach to body piercing than most other piercing studios. My staff and I continue to educate ourselves and seek new information. We believe in providing a large selection of quality, medical-grade jewelry to our customers. We travel several times a year to meet in person with our vendors in order to inspect and purchase their jewelry and talk to them about current trends in our market. We put time and money into training to help us be the best in the industry. I believe in sending my staff to seminars to continue their education in customer service and leadership, as well as piercing skills. I also provide my staff with books and audios to continue their personal development and their professional skills.

There are piercers out there who sell the twenty- or twenty-five-dollar piercing. This person is going to be putting a needle through your body; are you sure you want the cheapest piercing in town? Let me say that again: this person is going to be putting a needle through your body! For that price, don't expect to pick out your jewelry or receive expertise or any sort of customer service. We end up repiercing or changing jewelry on this type of piercing all the time. People go to a piercer because of the price. Often these piercers do okay on the piercing, but not consistently; too many people end up paying for repiercing by someone else, or they need to buy different jewelry because what they were pierced with was not correct.

Body piercing is a skill that in the overall picture of our society is very rare. There are very few body piercers, and of those, there are even fewer really good piercers. Even rarer are female piercers. I am very proud that in a male-dominated field I have succeeded above and beyond my own expectations.

All of the piercers who currently work for me are female. They have all been trained by me or by one of the body piercers that I have personally trained. They are all required to perform four hundred body piercings during their apprenticeship in order to become a certified body piercer. Every one of them looks like the girl next door. My piercers are very special, and they are all incredibly talented. They are also dignified and moral. Each one has been handpicked to pierce in my stores, starting out working sales then later being selected to pierce.

What I have learned in this business is that there is more to piercing than shoving a needle through the skin. It takes skill, experience, time, and patience to learn the art of body piercing. It takes great customer-service skills to become a great body piercer. As a body piercer, you work closely with your customers, and it is important to be compassionate, professional, and skillful. Our mission is to pierce our customers skillfully and professionally and to educate our clientele about body piercing so they have a good experience.

I could write a separate book about all the stories I have had customers tell me about their bad experiences with piercing. Piercers who are not correctly trained, who do not strive to be better piercers, and who have limited customer-service skills give the body-piercing industry a bad name. I have worked hard to create a good image of piercing in the communities where I work. I have made body piercing mainstream in my area, and I am extremely proud of that. I have proven that body piercing does not have to be a scary experience. You can be pierced at the mall, (yes, the mall!) in a clean and comfortable environment, by a person who treats you with respect. I am not saying that all piercing studios are bad. There are good ones out there, but they are few, and they fight the same battle that I do with less-reputable studios. I think a lot of piercing studios do not work hard enough to create a good image, and in this business, image is important.

My piercers and staff are not allowed to have more than two facial piercings. This seems contradictory to the field we are in, but we promote a certain image and work by a strict standard not to conform to the norm in the body-piercing industry. We do not do tattoos; we specialize in piercing, which is one of the reasons why we are the best at what we do.

I started out piercing at my store, Silver Safari, in Spokane, Washington, in 2000. In 2004, I opened Silver Safari at the Boulevard Mall in Las Vegas and pierced there for three years before moving that store to Bellingham, Washington. I have pierced live, on the air, on local radio stations, at a county fair, and at a local hot rod car show. I currently have two Silver Safari stores, one in Spokane, Washington, and the other in Bellingham, Washington. Both of my stores are in mainstream shopping malls. At my stores, we carry the largest selection of body jewelry in our area. We also sell sterling silver jewelry, semiprecious stone jewelry, and African wood carvings.

This is the most complete book ever written on the subject of body piercing. As you journey through my book, you will learn there is a lot that goes into body piercing. The information provided will guide you through each step of the piercing process. You will learn how to find a good piercer, know what size jewelry you should wear, and learn how to take proper care of your piercing. From the moment you leave the piercing studio, you will have the information you need to enjoy your piercing for years to come.

A glossary of terms is located at the back of this book.

Chapter One

How to Find a Piercing Shop

Where should you go to get pierced? This is a hard question to answer. Ask your friends where they got pierced. Did they have a good experience? Do they recommend the shop? I am still surprised by the number of people who go to piercers when they have heard negative comments about the piercer. Some people have negative experiences but then return to the same studio for another piercing. Many people make the decision based on price. Body piercing is an invasive procedure—do not make your decision based on price. What we see more often than you can believe is someone who went to the lowest-priced piercer and got a bad piercing. They end up in my store having to be repierced, and now they have paid for two piercings. Time and money could have been saved by researching and then choosing a reputable piercer. I believe in the saying, "You get what you pay for." If you cannot afford to go to the piercer who is your first choice, wait until you have the money saved up. Being patient can save you a lot of frustration and enable you to have the best piercing experience possible.

When you are ready to get a piercing visit piercing studios, and keep in mind that you do not have to get pierced that day. Make time to do your research! Go to several shops and look around. Ask yourself: Is it clean? Is the staff friendly and knowledgeable? Trust your instincts: do you feel comfortable there? Ask about sterilization: do they use an autoclave to sterilize their needles? Needles must be autoclaved and then disposed of after each piercing. How do they sterilize their jewelry? Jewelry does not necessarily have to be autoclaved to be sterilized. There are cold sterilization methods using hospital-grade sterilants that work well to sterilize jewelry (such as Wavacide). This is important because there are some types of jewelry that cannot be autoclaved. Ask if the piercing shop autoclaves their tools. Tools that are used in piercing have blood on them, and it is crucial that they are put through an autoclave to be sterilized. Does the piercing shop use only medical-grade jewelry? Do they use the needles only one time? It makes me sick to my stomach that you would even have to ask that, but I know of a piercer who used the same needle on three sisters while their Dad watched instead of pulling his girls out of there! It's okay to stand up and say, "I don't want to be pierced here, I've changed my mind. Please give me my money back, because I'd like to leave!" Finally, be sure to ask them if they reuse their jewelry. I have heard of a piercing shop where you can trade in the jewelry that you were pierced with. They autoclave the piercing jewelry and reuse it. Piercing jewelry is being inserted into your body—it should be new.

In the introduction to this book, I discussed freehand piercing and piercing using clamps. The only piercings a clamp or Tuttle Tweezer (and I recommend a Tuttle Tweezer rather than a clamp) should be used on would be the tongue, lip, and tragus, because these piercings require a tool to hold the body part during the piercing. All other piercings should be done without the use of these tools.

I have seen piercers wrap a rubber band around a clamp to hold it closed, too tightly clamping the tool on the body part they are piercing. When investigating piercing shops before getting a piercing, be sure to ask if they do this. If a piercer needs to use a rubber band because he or she does not know how to properly hold a clamp or Tuttle Tweezer with the right amount of pressure to keep the tool on the tongue, lip, or tragus, you should find another piercing shop.

We repeatedly hear customers who were pierced with a clamp say that the clamp hurt more than the piercing. When they find out that we don't pierce that way, they become our customer for life. If the correct amount of pressure is applied using a clamp or Tuttle Tweezer, meaning the pressure is controlled by the piercer, not with the use of a rubber band or by locking the clamp, the customer should not feel the effect of the tool.

Be sure to ask how long the piercers have been working or how many piercings they have done. Keep in mind that even if piercers are fairly new, they will still be good piercers if they have received good training. We have had piercers from other shops tell us that their training and apprenticeship consisted of them watching another piercer for one week, and then they started piercing with no supervision. Feel free to ask piercers what their training involved and how long it lasted.

Ask if you will get written care instructions and care solution with your piercing. Do you get to pick out the jewelry you will be pierced with? I see people all the time who come in wearing this great big jewelry that is not the right size for their piercing. There is no reason to pierce with larger gauge jewelry than what is necessary unless the customer specifically asks for it.

Most customers have no idea what gauge, length, or diameter they should be pierced with. They depend on the expertise of the piercer or the staff at the studio to choose the right size for them. I have seen countless nose piercings with gigantic nose screws. These people usually say that was all the piercer had, but they went through with the piercing even though they did not like the jewelry.

It's common to see piercing studios carry only basic body-piercing jewelry, which is surgical steel with steel beads; this is the least expensive jewelry for a piercer to purchase. Most people prefer to start out with jewelry that has stones on it, so it looks good to them, and they are willing to pay extra for the jewelry they like.

We strive to give customers more than they pay for by providing a large selection of jewelry to choose from, giving a bottle of care solution with the piercing, giving written care instructions, and offering topical anesthetic (numbing gel or numbing spray) at no extra charge. We are also available for unlimited consultations before and after the piercing. There are piercing studios that offer care solution and topical anesthetic for an additional fee, which is better than not having it available at all.

If there is no choice or if you do not like the jewelry, move on to the next shop. If the studio is too cheap to carry a variety of piercing jewelry, they may also be too cheap to provide you with a quality piercing. It is very important for the studio to provide a selection of medical-grade piercing jewelry other than surgical steel because some people are allergic to surgical steel. Different types of medical-grade jewelry should include titanium, 14 kt gold, polycarbonate, and Bioflex.

As I stated earlier, some shops offer very inexpensive piercings. If the price of the piercing is incredibly cheap, you need to ask yourself why.

Do your research so that you will not regret your decision later on.

Tip: Questions to ask when looking for a piercing studio.
- Do they autoclave their needles?
- Are needles used only one time and disposed of?
- Do they autoclave their tools?
- How is the jewelry sterilized?
- Do they use medical-grade jewelry?
- Do you get to choose your jewelry?
- Do they offer jewelry other than surgical steel?
- Do they pierce freehand or with a clamp?
- Will you receive written care instructions?
- What is recommended for aftercare and will you receive care solution or is it available to purchase?
- How long has the piercer been piercing and/or how many piercings have they performed?
- Who trained them and how long was their training?
- Is licensing required by the state, and if so, do the shop and piercers have the required licenses to pierce?

I cannot emphasize enough the importance of doing your research. Do not be in such a hurry to get a piercing that you go to any shop that is available. Make sure you choose a good place to be pierced.

When you do make the decision of where you will be pierced, be sure you are comfortable with the entire process, from start to finish. If at any time you are uncomfortable with your piercer or the environment of the piercing shop, or if you feel the piercing is not being performed in a sterile manner, stand up, ask for your money back, and leave. You do not need to sit through a piercing you are having second thoughts about because you do not want to hurt somebody's feelings; you are never going to see this person again. You need to ask yourself what is more important, the piercer's feelings or your body and well-being? Get up and leave, it's that simple.

Many people have asked me *after* I've pushed the needle through if we sterilize the needle and only use it once. Don't be afraid to ask this question; we are not offended by it. We also receive calls from people who were pierced at another shop but were not given instructions on how to care for their new piercing. Again, when researching where to get pierced, ask about aftercare before the piercing is done, and make sure you are comfortable with what is recommended.

I have had girls tell me that their piercer was stoned or smelled like alcohol, and they wanted to leave, but they were scared and did not know what to do, so they went through with it. I have also had girls tell me that while they were having their belly button pierced, the piercer had a cigarette hanging out of his lip and ashes were falling on their stomach. Remember the dad who told me that a piercer used the same needle on all three of his girls? Your safety and well-being are the most important issues.

There are piercers who set up a piercing shop in their homes. If you are considering being pierced in a home environment, check with your state to see what the law is regarding this. Although rare, some states will allow a shop to be set up in a home, but very specific requirements must be met. Because it could be easy for a piercer to be lax in a home setting, it may not always be the best environment for a piercing. If a separate room is set up and follows all applicable guidelines, it could be worth investigating. We have heard many horror stories of self-trained piercers who, with little experience, pierce out of their home; their customers end up in my stores. In every case, the customer went to that piercer because his or her price for a piercing was extremely cheap. Exercise caution in choosing your piercer.

Situations like these happen far too often in states where body-piercing laws are limited or nonexistent. I have concerns about laws not being strong enough in some states, but I am also concerned that in other states laws are too restrictive for body piercers. The problem is that often people making the laws know nothing about body piercing. In Las Vegas, body piercers are heavily regulated by the health department. They send people out to inspect us who know nothing about piercing. They enforce laws that they do not understand. They make us abide by laws they cannot explain. They focus on sterilization, but not at all on training.

Oregon has very strict laws for body piercers, right down to the point that the state dictates what the body piercers have to tell customers to use for aftercare. They do not allow body piercers to recommend or sell any care products. Even though I am committed to only one aftercare product, I am open-minded enough to realize that not every product will work for every person. In this regard, a state dictating that only one type of aftercare can be used makes no sense.

The state of Washington recently adopted its first laws regarding body piercing. I am proud that I was able to attend the committee meetings in Olympia and offer input to make common-sense laws. Through this process, I saw firsthand the many different viewpoints among piercers. Our body-piercing regulations in Washington are tied together with tattoo and cosmetic tattooing. This, along with different perspectives of the industry, created many heated debates. While I do not agree with all the regulations that were implemented, I am pleased that I was able to see the process of how the laws are formed.

CHAPTER TWO

Appropriate Age

A twelve-year-old girl who had her tongue pierced came into one of my stores. Twelve years old! The week before, her mom brought her in to be pierced, and we turned her away, so her mother took her to a shop up the street where they willingly pierced her. Should age be a factor? Yes, absolutely! The age debate is never ending in the world of body piercing.

Some states regulate the age a minor has to be to get a piercing. In Nevada and Washington, where I have pierced, there are no laws on age, so it is up to the body piercer to determine their own policy on this. In Nevada, a parent is required to sign for a minor child. In Washington, there is no law, although at my stores, we do require a parent's written consent. I have also pierced in Idaho, where the law allows minors age fourteen and older to be pierced with a parent's consent.

When I first started piercing, I would not do body piercing on anyone under sixteen. What happened is this: moms would bring in their thirteen-, fourteen-, and fifteen-year-olds to be pierced. I would turn them away, and the moms would say to me, "Genia, I really want you to do it. If you won't, then I will take them to another place that will, and I don't want to do that." Well, I turned them away for a while, and guess what happened? Some of these same people would come back with bad piercings and all sorts of problems that I would end up fixing anyway; so they broke me down. I think thirteen is a good age—teenagers are old enough and responsible enough to care for their piercings and their bodies are developed enough.

One could argue that this age is too young for someone to be pierced; the minor may not be responsible enough to care for the piercing. We always make sure the parent is present to hear the care instructions with their child. There will always be some minors who are not responsible enough to care for their piercings, and they will end up having problems— but the same can be said for adults.

I started piercing minors who were age thirteen or older so that I would have the peace of mind that they would:

- receive a good piercing
- be educated on how to take care of their piercing
- receive care products to use on their new piercing

The Association of Professional Piercers (APP)[1] sets stringent standards for piercers who join the membership of their organization and on their website are recommendations for piercees; see safepiercing.org for more information. While I do not agree with all of the standards set forth by the APP, they are the one organization trying to set a standard for the industry. They take a strong stand against piercing the nipples of anyone under the age of eighteen. I personally do not understand why anyone under eighteen would need to have their nipples pierced, and I agree they should not have it done. The reality is that sometimes they want it, and their parents will give their consent. It is not legal in every state to pierce the nipples of minors, even with parental consent. I have a real struggle with this issue, because when we turn them away, they go up the street to "The Shop of Despair" (as I like to call the shops that will pierce anyone at any age, with or without parental consent, and do not care if they do it right). A large number of these people come back to my store because the piercing was not done right, they did not like how they were treated, or they were having a problem with their piercing.

If you are under eighteen and want a nipple piercing, be patient and wait until you are eighteen to get it. In some states, piercing the nipples of minors falls into the category of an offense against a minor. The best recommendation for female nipple piercing is to have it done after you are finished having babies, which is discussed in more detail later in this book.

We have had parents request body piercings on their young children. It always amazes me the lack of common sense some people have. We have seen young children with body piercings that should never have been done. If you are a parent, please be patient when it comes to your child's body piercing. The child needs to be not only physically developed but also mature enough to handle and care for the piercing on his or her own.

---

1   Association of Professional Piercers (safepiercing.org).

> **Tip:** The best ages for piercing minors.
> - Six months and older—earlobes only with piercing guns
> - Thirteen years and up for cartilage piercings with guns
> - Thirteen years and up for above-the-waist piercings
> - Eighteen years and up for nipple, genital, surface, and dermal-anchor piercings

When we were deciding where to open our second store, we called piercing studios in the cities we were interested in to inquire about what age they started piercing belly buttons. One piercer told us to bring our daughter in, and he would look at her to determine if she should be pierced or not, and he did not care about her age. We have no idea what he would have based his decision on.

The National Conference of State Legislatures[2] website has the most complete listing of state laws for piercing minors that I have been able to find. Although this is not a complete list, there are provisions for most states.

Ear-piercing guns and piercing the ears of children will be discussed in detail in the chapters ahead.

---

2   National Conference of State Legislatures, The Forum for America's Ideas, www. ncsl.org/programs/health/minorbodyart.htm.

CHAPTER THREE

Will the Body Always Accept a Piercing?

When the body is pierced and a foreign object (jewelry) is inserted into the body, it is the body's natural reaction to try to push the foreign object out. What will help the body to accept the piercing is to pierce with the correct gauge and type of body jewelry. It is also very important to make sure enough skin is pierced to begin with. If a piercing is done with jewelry that is too thin in gauge, the body can easily reject it. If not enough skin is pierced, the body will most likely reject that too.

The healthier the body is, the faster and better the piercing will heal. Taking care of the piercing properly while it is healing will also help, and this is discussed further in the chapters that follow. Changing the jewelry too early can cause the piercing to become irritated or infected and could possibly lead to losing the piercing.

There is no guarantee that the body will accept any piercing.

Tip: Help your body accept a piercing.
- Always get pierced with the correct gauge and type of jewelry.
- Make sure enough skin is pierced, since shallow piercings tend to grow out.
- Take proper care of the piercing while it is healing.
- Good nutrition will help keep the body healthier.
- Avoid stress.
- Do not change the jewelry until the piercing is completely healed.

If you get a piercing and not enough skin was pierced, return to your piercer immediately and ask him or her to look at it (do not take the jewelry out). The piercer needs to see the piercing with the jewelry in, to determine if the piercing is too shallow. If it is, the jewelry should be removed, and allow the piercing to heal for at least two weeks before repiercing. Although piercers have different policies, there should be no charge for this.

CHAPTER FOUR

Gauge and Length Conversion Chart

When it comes to gauges, the larger the number, the thinner the bar or hoop will be. Some body jewelry is measured in millimeters and some is measured by the gauge or inch.

Below is a chart that shows the conversion of the thickness of the jewelry from gauge to millimeter and the length of the jewelry from inches to millimeters.

Thickness:		Length:	
Gauge	**Millimeter**	**Inches**	**Millimeter**
14g	1.6 mm	1/4″	6 mm
12g	2 mm	5/16″	8 mm
10g	2.5 mm	3/8″	10 mm
8g	3.2 mm	7/16″	11 mm
6g	4 mm	1/2″	12 mm
4g	5 mm	9/16″	14 mm
2g	6.5 mm	5/8″	16 mm
0g	8 mm	3/4″	19 mm
00g	10 mm	7/8″	22 mm
7/16″	11 mm	1″	25 mm
½″	12 mm	1–1/4″	32 mm
9/16″	14 mm	1–3/8″	35 mm
5/8″	16 mm	1–1/2″	38 mm

¾"	19 mm	1–3/4"	44 mm
7/8"	22 mm	2"	51 mm
1"	25 mm		
1–1/4"	30 mm		
1–1/2"	38 mm		
1–5/8"	41 mm		
1–3/4"	44 mm		
2"	50 mm		

CHAPTER FIVE

Length and Diameter Chart for Hoops and Barbells

Hoops are measured from side to side, straight across the inside of the hoop. Barbells are measured from the length of the bar—the beads are not measured. The following chart shows the diameters and lengths of available body jewelry.

Hoop, barbell, and labret, measured in inches:

Hoop Diameters	Barbell Lengths	Labret Lengths	Navel Bar Lengths	Eyebrow Bar Lengths
1/4	1/4	1/4	3/8	1/4
5/16	5/16	5/16	7/16	5/16
3/8	3/8	3/8	1/2	3/8
7/16	7/16	7/16	5/8	
1/2	1/2	1/2		
9/16	5/8			
5/8	3/4			
3/4	7/8			
7/8	1			
1	1/1/4			
1–1/2	1–1/2			
	1–3/4			
	2			

CHAPTER SIX

Size Chart

This chart illustrates how to measure jewelry and provides examples of the difference in size between gauge and length. Please note this chart is not to scale and is offered only as a reference.

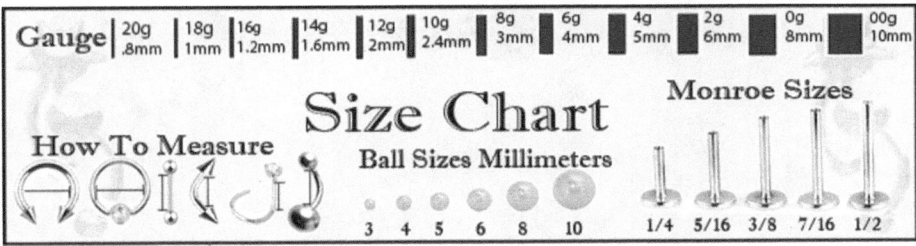

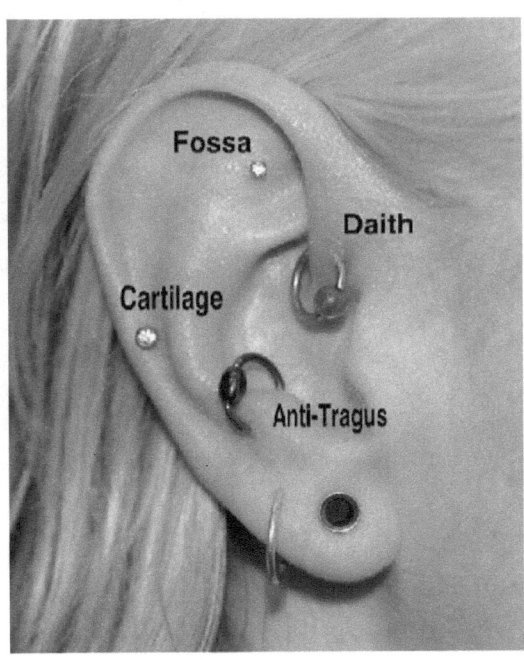

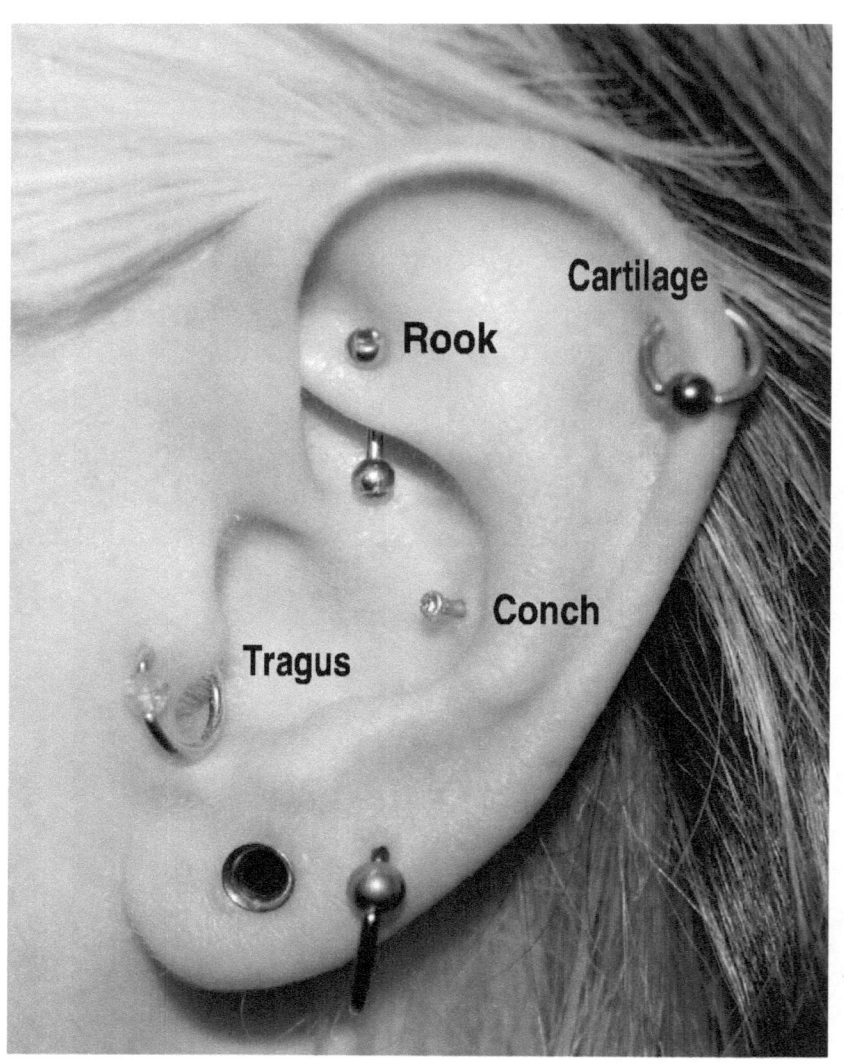

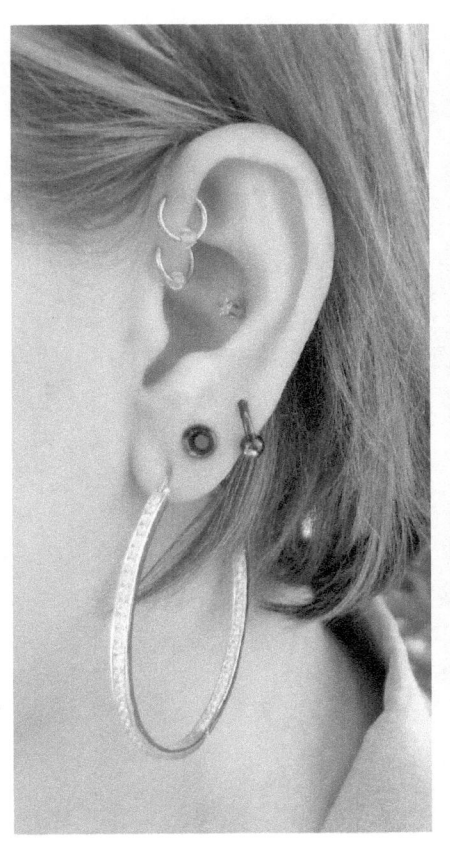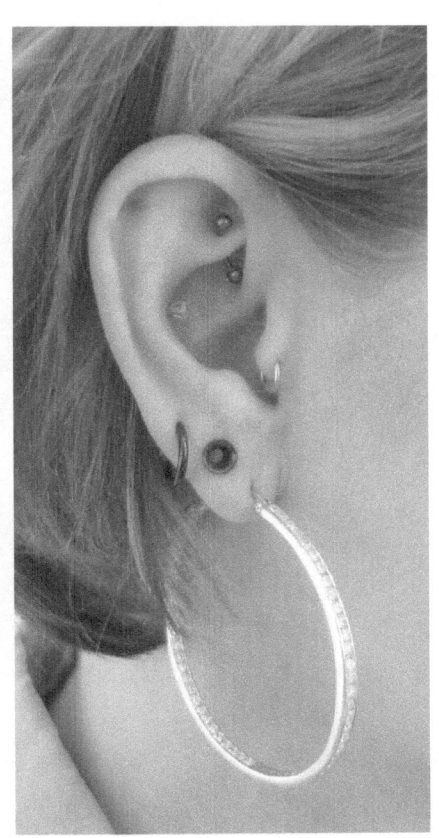

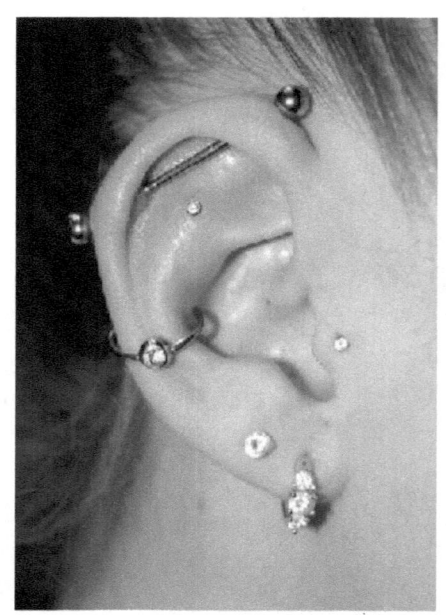

Industrial Ear Piercing, Fossa, Conch, Tragus

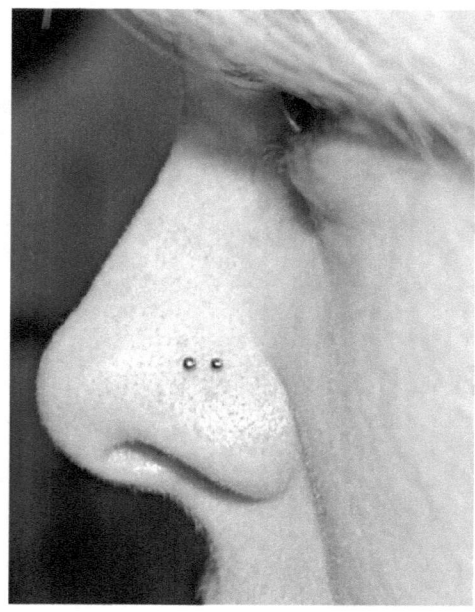

Double Nose Piercing

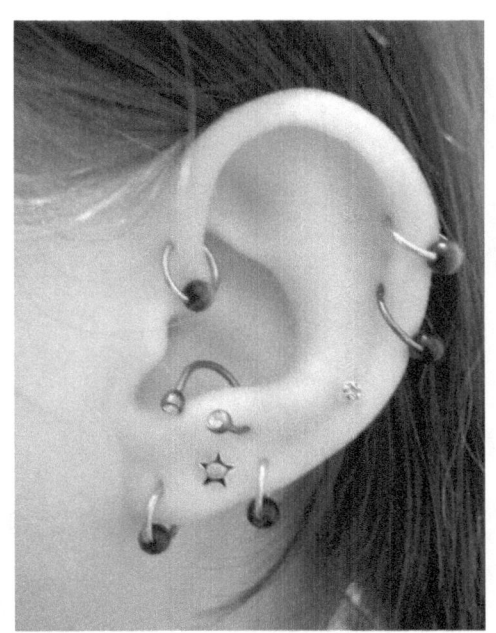

Daith, Anti-Tragus

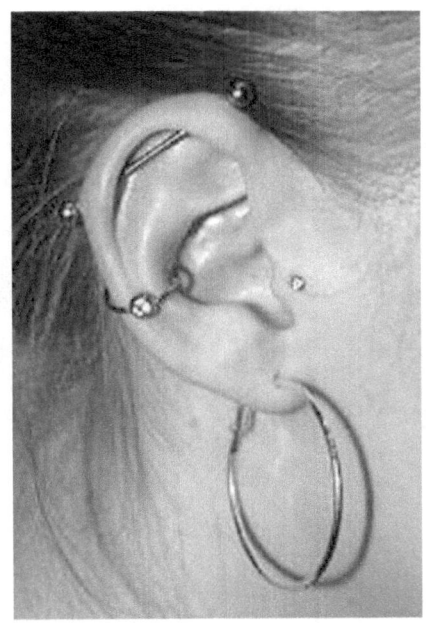

Industrial, Conch, Tragus

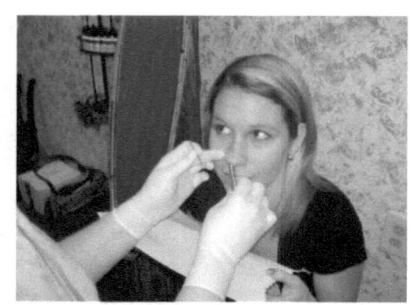

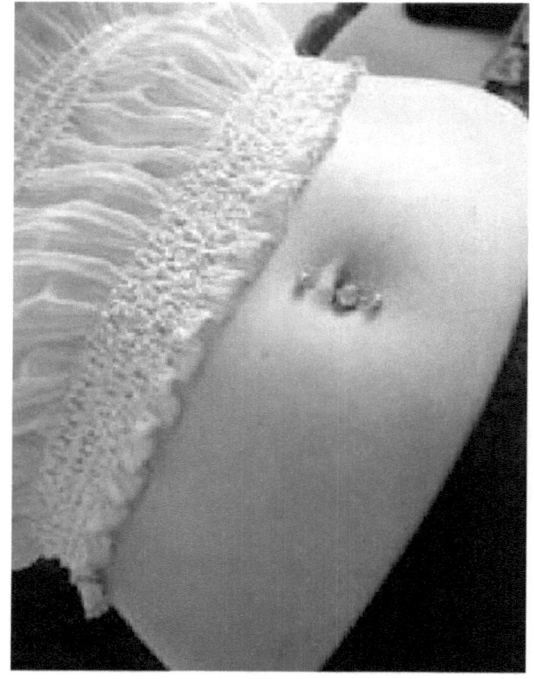

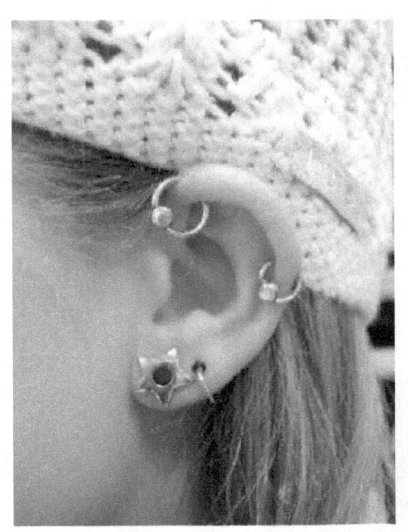

Industrial piercing with 14 gauge hoops

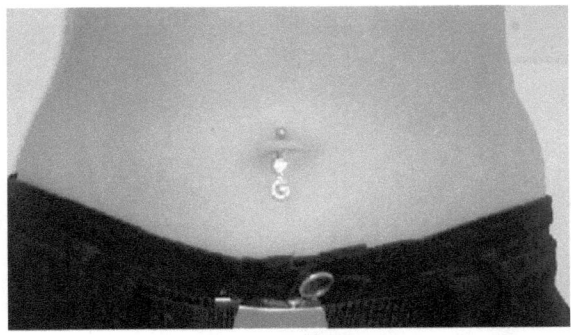

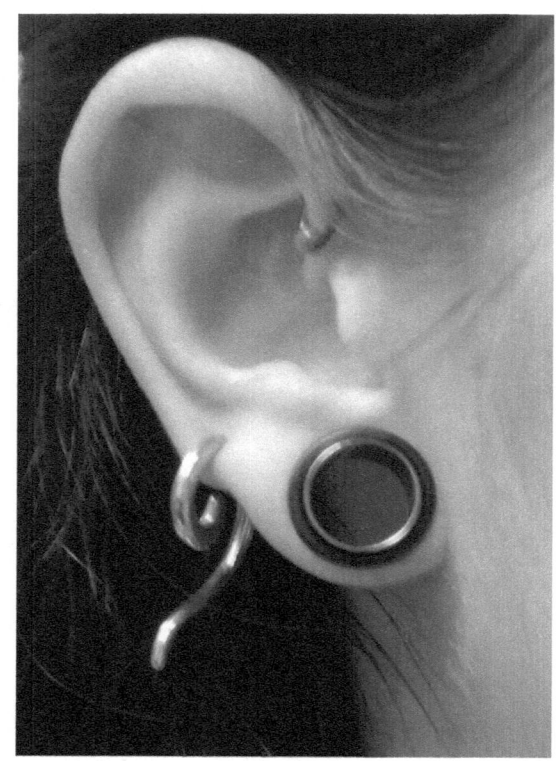

Daith, gauged ear

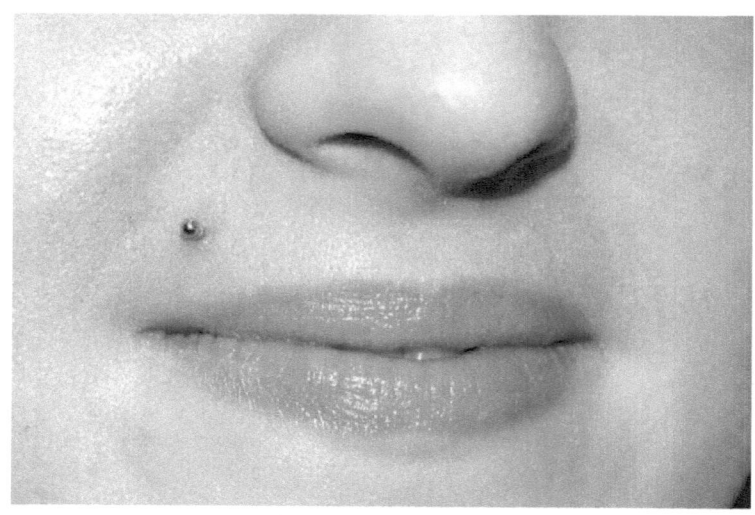

Marilyn Monroe Beauty Mark

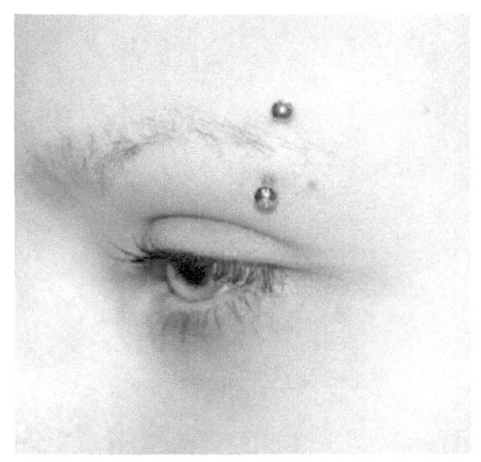

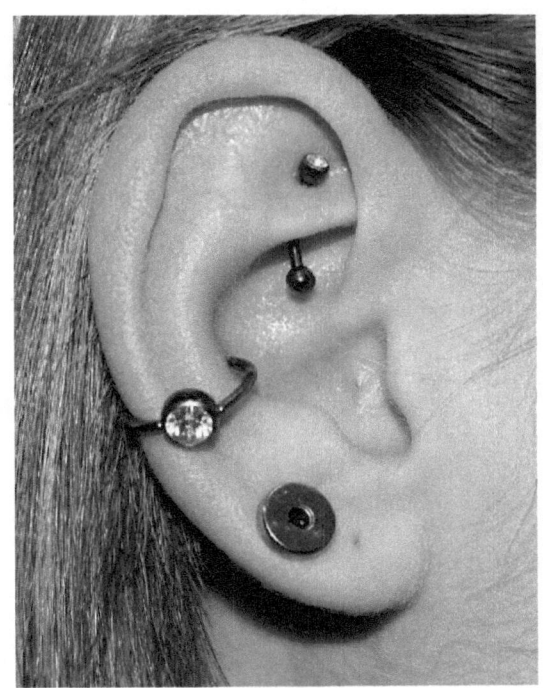

Rook, Conch, second hole gauged

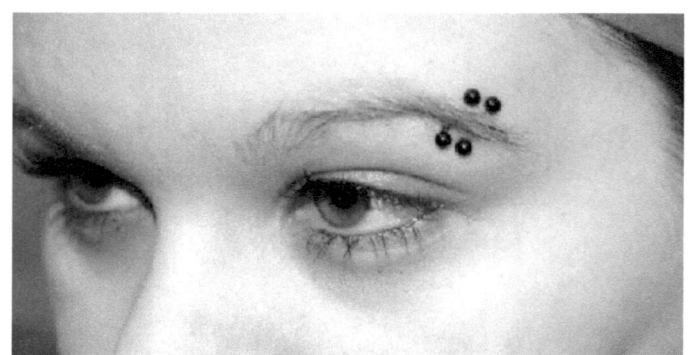

Double Eyebrow piercing

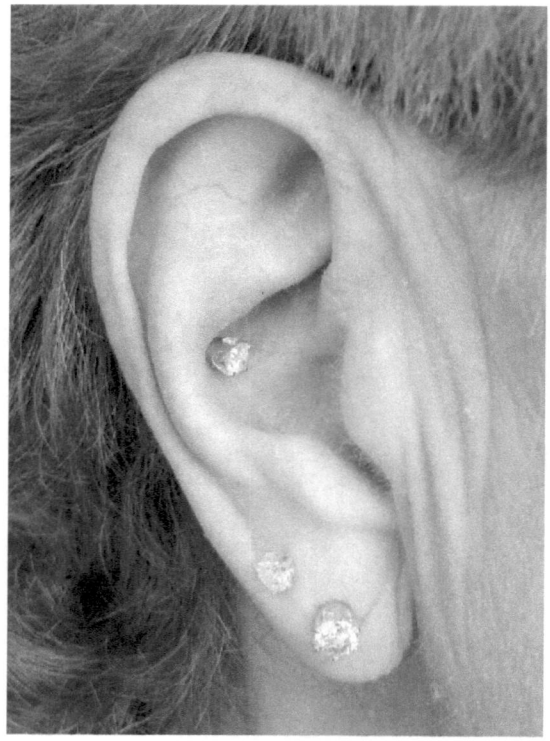

Conch Piercing

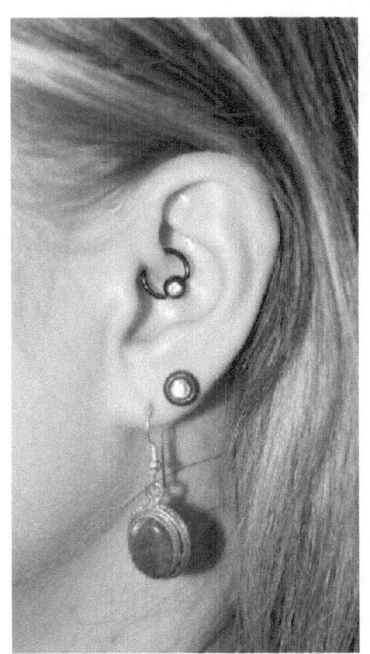

Inside Daith Piercing

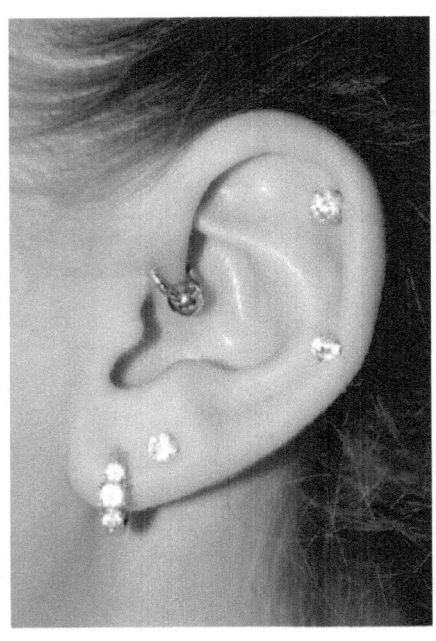

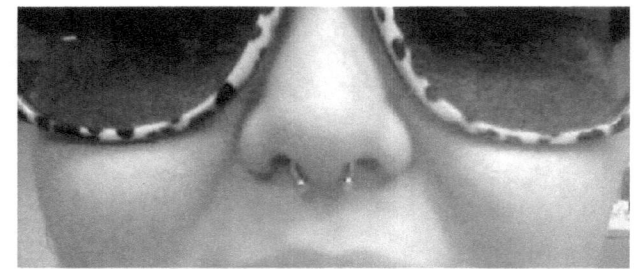

Septum piercing

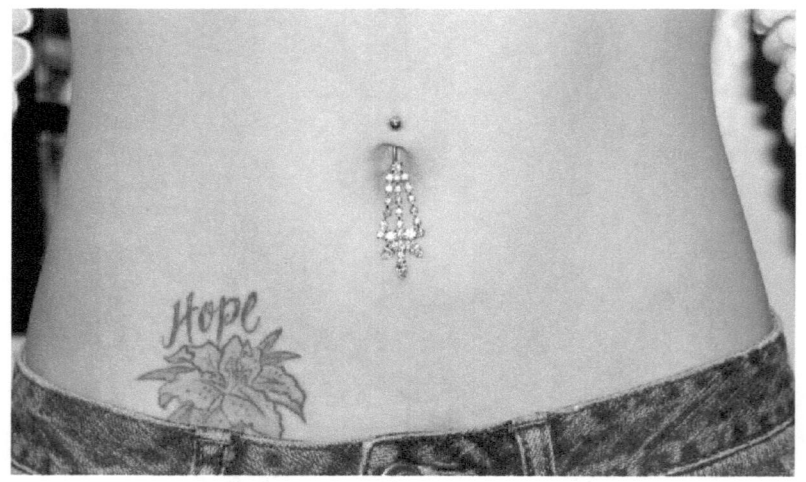

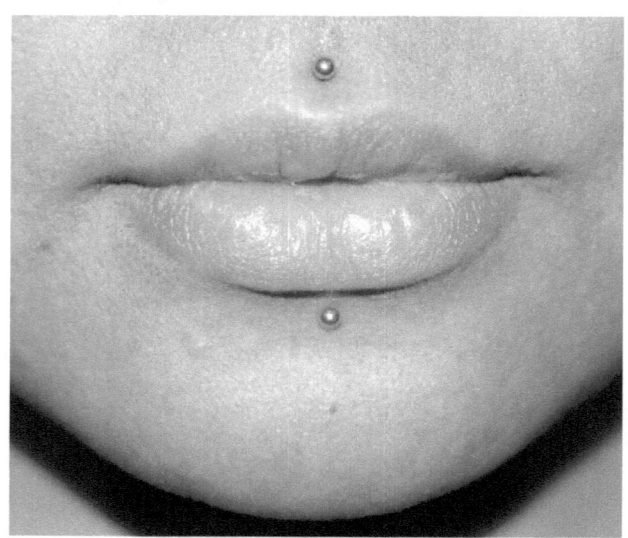

Medusa and Labret

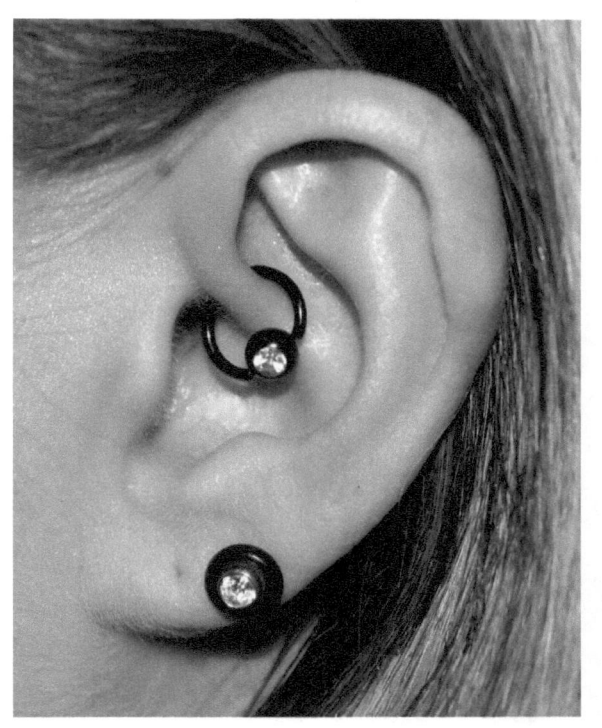

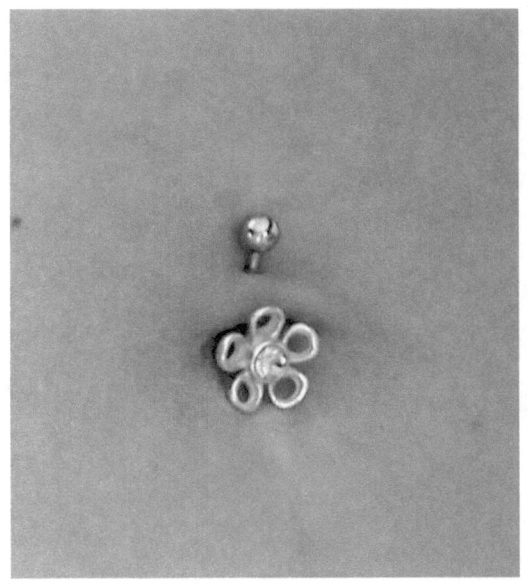

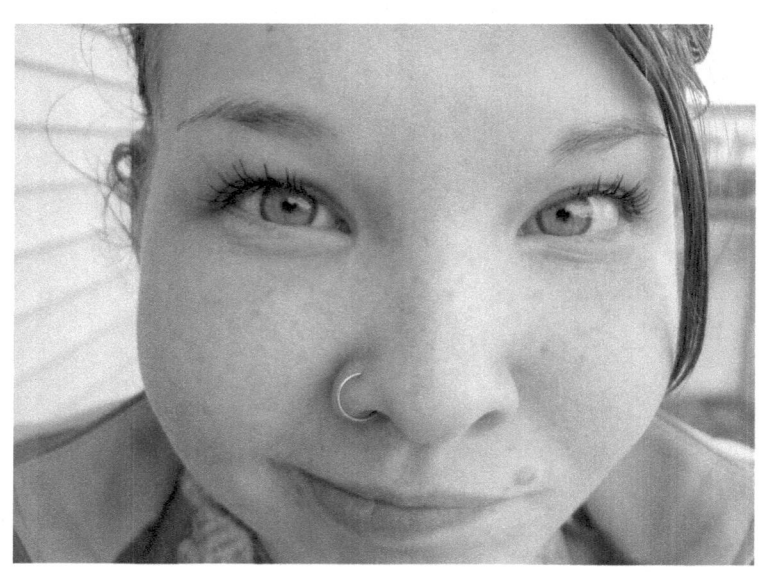

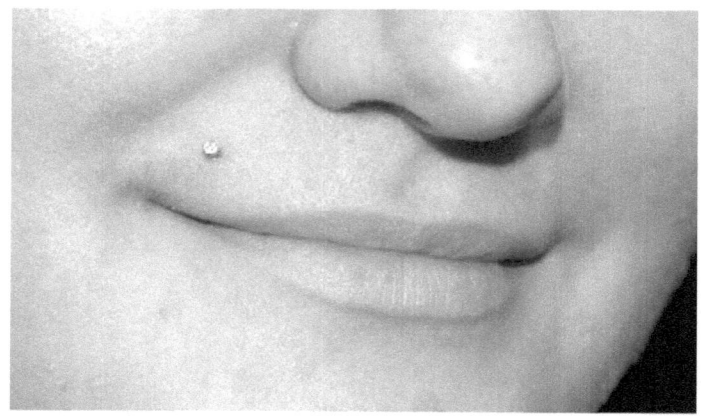

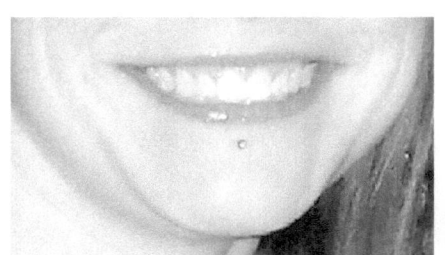

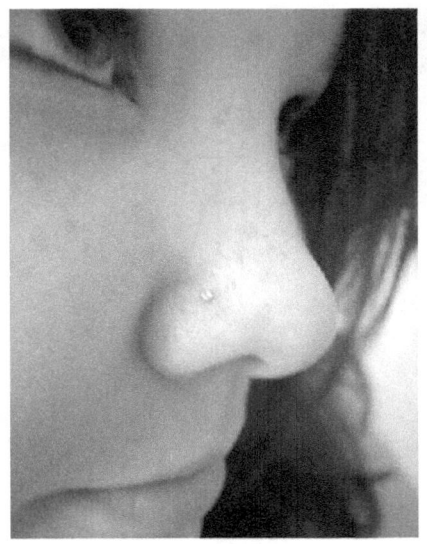

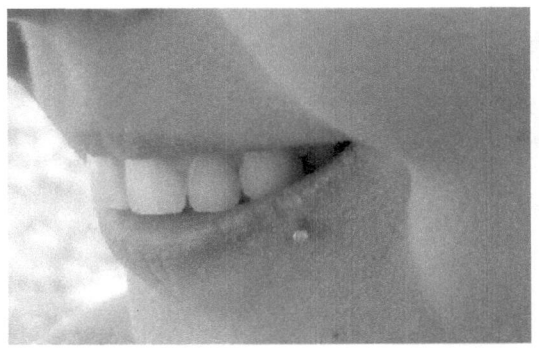

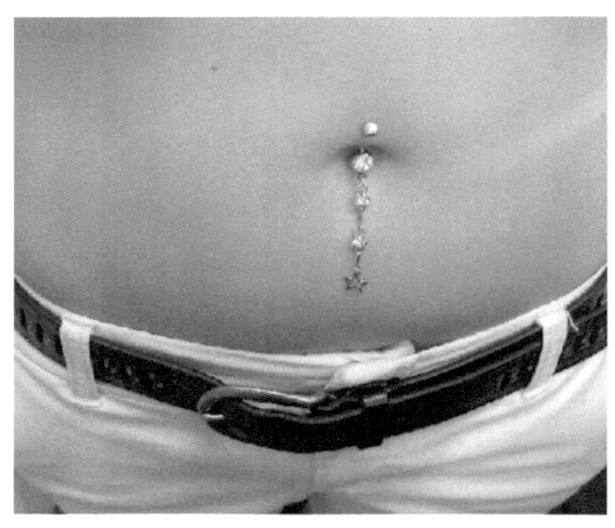

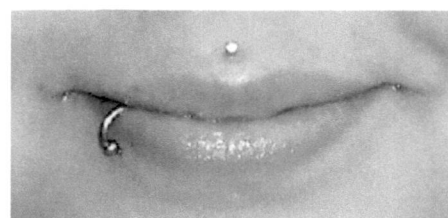

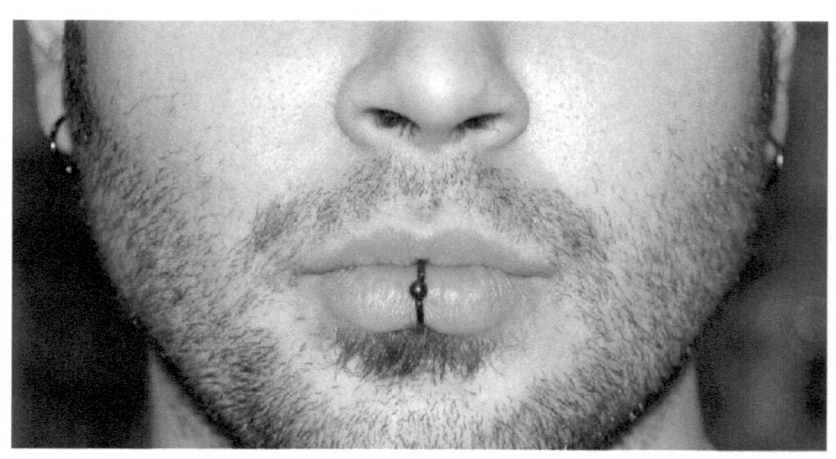

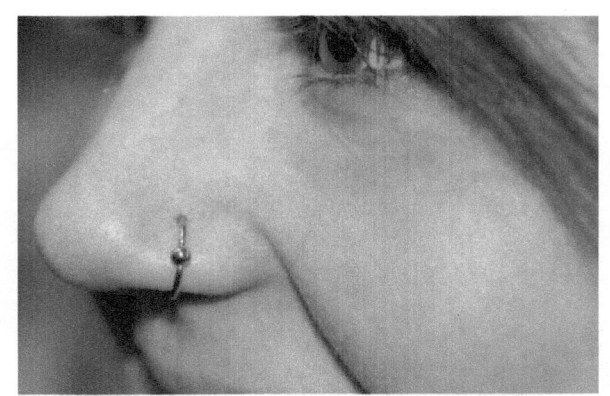

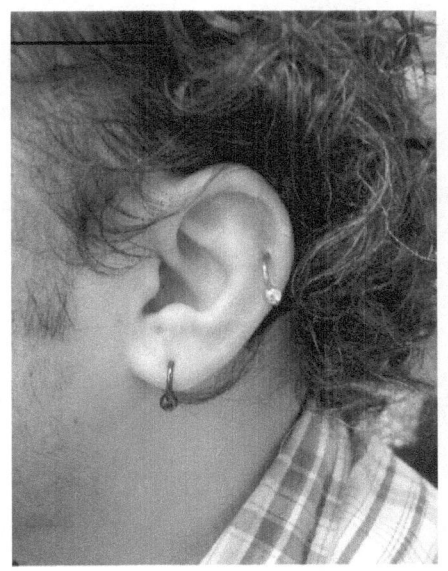

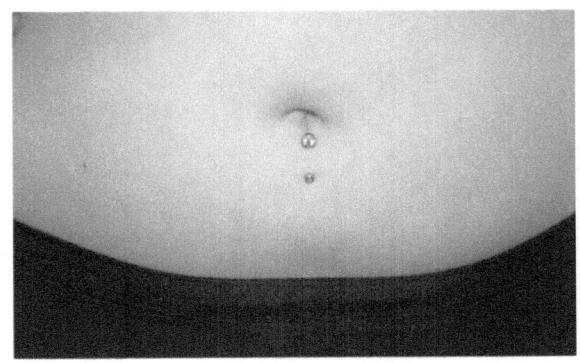

Lower Navel Piercing

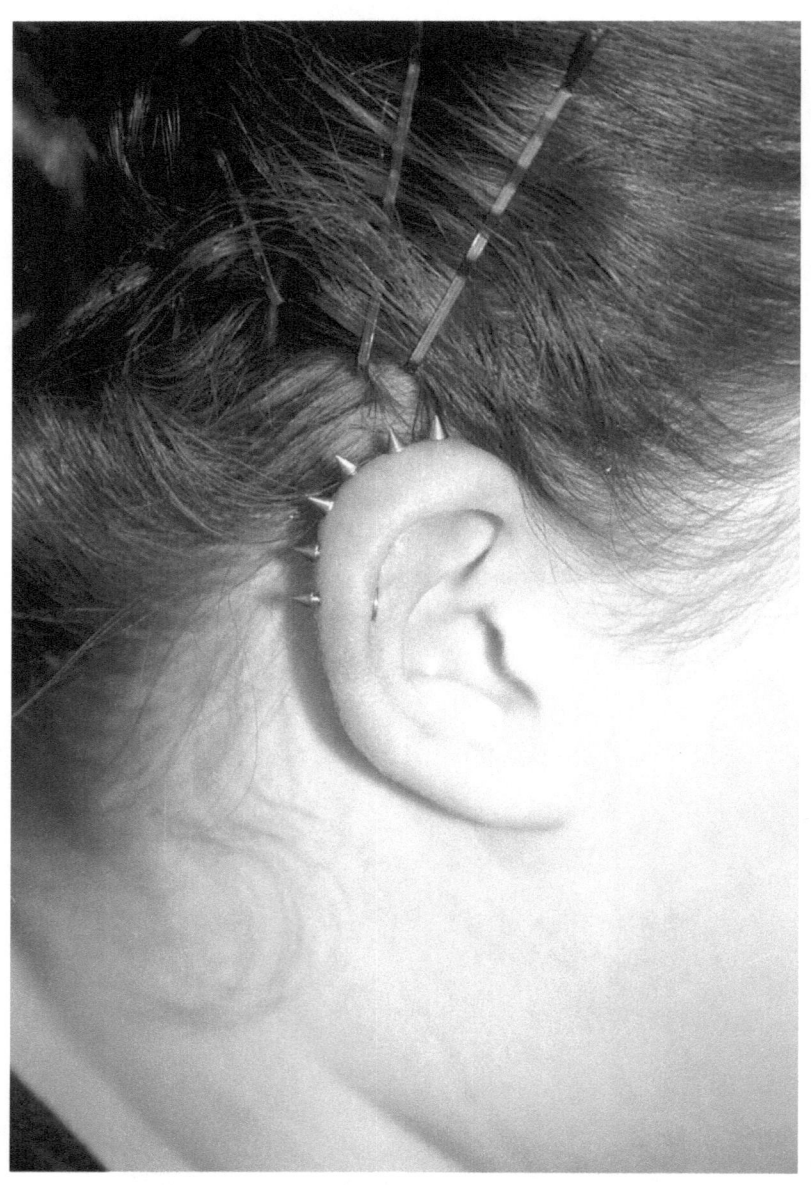

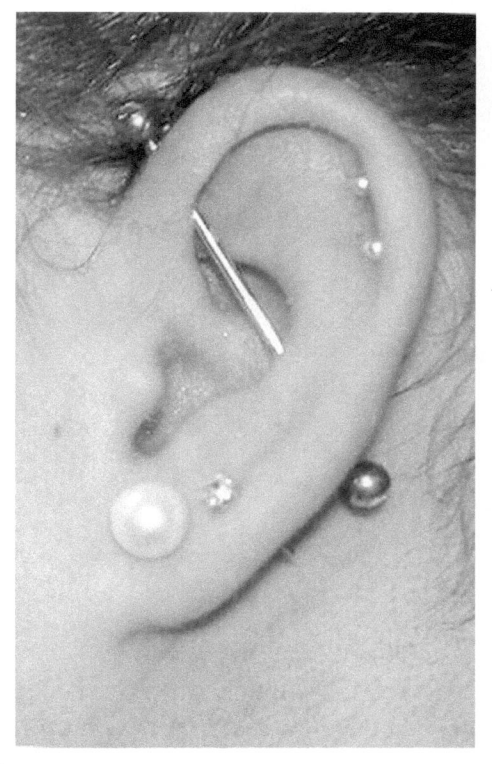

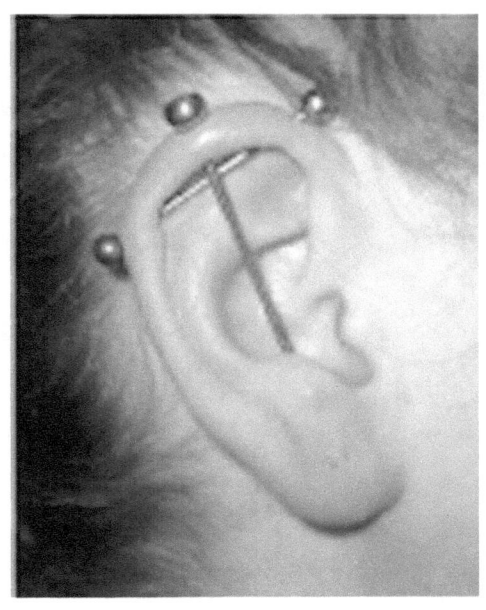

PHOTOGRAPHS TAKEN BY
JOANNA SCHLOSSER, DENNIS SULLIVAN,
CHAD GAFFANEY, AND GENIA GAFFANEY

CHAPTER SEVEN

Choosing Surgical Steel, Titanium, or Gold

There is a great variety of jewelry to choose from for your initial piercing. The days of only piercing with surgical steel are gone. We now have choices, which make it even more fun to get that new piercing. It's important for the safety of the piercing and for proper healing to be pierced with jewelry that is specifically made for piercing. The appropriate materials include surgical steel, titanium, polycarbonate, gold, and Bioflex.

Medical-Grade Surgical Steel (316L)

Surgical steel is by far the most popular metal and it has the most styles to choose from. The only drawback with surgical steel is that it has trace amounts of nickel in it, which some people are allergic to.

Medical-Grade Titanium
(6AL4V ELI, Grade 2-Pure Unalloyed Titanium)

There is pure titanium jewelry (6AL4V ELI, Grade 2-Pure Unalloyed Titanium) and anodized titanium (titanium plating over surgical steel). I only recommend pure titanium for piercing. I have found that people who have metal allergies and cannot wear surgical steel have great success with pure titanium. People do well with titanium because it is the least reactive metal to the body; it is what is used in hip and knee implants. I do not use plated or anodized bars or hoops (titanium plating over surgical steel) because the acid in a person's system can remove the titanium plating and expose the new piercing to a surgical steel bar. This will cause an immediate reaction if that person is allergic to surgical steel. Since new piercings tend to be fairly acidic, it is crucial not to use titanium-plated jewelry for piercing. Titanium in its natural state is light gray but is popular because of its brilliant color that can be achieved through an electrochemical (heat) process. Although it is a strong metal, titanium is lightweight and comfortable to wear. It resists corrosion and does not react to most acids.

Hermetical Gold

This metal is made using an advanced process that gold plates surgical steel. The process is used to treat dental implants, bone implants, and surgical instruments. The finish is pure 24 kt gold over 316L surgical steel. Pure 24 kt gold is more easily accepted by the body than surgical steel because it does not contain nickel. I love this jewelry because the gold plating does not come off, and the body will not come into contact with the surgical steel. The benefit of this type of jewelry is that you have the look of gold but retain the strength of the surgical steel. This is a great choice for anyone with sensitive skin. Another great benefit of pure 24 kt gold is that it will not tarnish like 14 kt gold. Hermetical gold is not to be confused with standard gold-plated body jewelry, which will not always hold its finish. The acid in a person's system will generally remove standard gold plating, leaving one with a surgical steel bar. The hermetical gold comes with a lifetime guarantee. This type of jewelry can be used in all piercings. We use it mostly for nose piercings and ear piercings. It is also more cost effective than 14 kt gold.

Jewelers-Grade Hypoallergenic 14 kt Gold

Some people can only wear gold; their body will not accept anything else. The gold body jewelry is beautiful, although it can be expensive. When wearing 14 kt gold jewelry, it is important to keep in mind that it does tarnish. It reacts to the acids in the system, causing the metal to tarnish. Gold jewelry should be cleaned occasionally with a good gold jewelry dip, available from most jewelers at the mall. Use a small soft brush to clean the stones to keep them shiny. Be sure to rinse well under running water to remove all the cleaner before inserting jewelry back into the piercing. Gold is a soft metal, so take care to treat it gently. Because gold does tarnish, it does not autoclave well; it comes out of the autoclave looking dark.

Polycarbonate

This is a great choice for anyone who has metal allergies. It is more flexible than acrylic, is hypoallergenic, and can be autoclaved. It is a popular choice for tongue piercing because it is available with a flat top and it is transparent. This is a good choice for the initial piercing for those who need to hide their tongue piercing. I have only found one company that carries this product.

Bioflex

This is implant grade and completely autoclavable. It is called different names by different manufactures, such as Bioflex, Bioplastic, Bioplast, etc. Its look is similar to polycarbonate. It is popular because it is transparent and comfortable because it is flexible. It can be used in any piercing. It is also a great choice for those who have metal allergies. What I love about Bioflex labret bars is that they are available with metal beads and stones so it has the look of a metal piece of jewelry with the comfort of Bioflex inside the lip. I also like that the stone, ball, or spike snaps tight inside the bar so there is no worry about a bead coming unscrewed. I prefer using screw on beads for the initial piercing and snap-in beads only for healed piercings. This is because the snap in beads can be harder to remove if there is a problem with the new piercing.

Niobium

This jewelry is also good quality and can be used in piercing (it looks similar to titanium), but I don't use it because it reacts easily to the acids in the system which makes the color fade off. It is not a favorite among customers because it does not hold its color well.

I do *not* recommend piercing with the following types of jewelry:

Acrylic

Acrylic jewelry is never recommended for any new piercing because overtightening the beads can strip the threads, and then the bead will not stay on. It is not worth the risk of losing the piercing. I had one person tell me that she had her navel pierced with a piece of acrylic jewelry and the jewelry was defective. The acrylic bar broke while it was in her new piercing. I only recommend acrylic jewelry for a healed piercing. Even for healed piercings, I am not a fan of acrylic jewelry or steel bars with acrylic beads. They are popular because of the price and a lot of people like wearing acrylic beads for their tongue piercing because if they bite down on the bead, it is easier on their teeth than metal beads.

Anodized Titanium

This is titanium plating over surgical steel and should not be used for piercing. The acid in a body's system can wear the plating off exposing the surgical steel bar.

Gold-Plated

Jewelry which has gold plating over surgical steel should never be used in piercing. The thin layer of gold wears away quickly, exposing the steel bar underneath. Gold-plated jewelry is viewed as costume jewelry, not quality karat gold jewelry.

Organic Body Jewelry

Organic jewelry such as bone, horn, wood, and stone should be worn only in healed piercings.

PTFE (Polytetrafluoroethylene)

This is a flexible plastic material used to make tongue and navel bars, as well as longer bars for surface piercings. It is self-threading, so all you have to do is cut the PTFE with a razor blade to the length needed, and screw the beads onto the bar. PTFE is trademarked under several different names, most commonly known as Teflon.[3] Teflon, when heated is known to cause serious health risks. Although the PTFE used for body jewelry is not heated (unless it is autoclaved), I will not recommend it to my customers.

---

3   "What Teflon Is And Why You Should Avoid It," *The Good Human* (Dec. 2, 2008):
http://www.thegoodhuman.com/2007/07/31/what-teflon-is-and-why-you-should-avoid-it.

CHAPTER EIGHT

Piercing with the Correct Gauge and Length

B ody jewelry that works for one person may not work for another. It is extremely important to pierce with jewelry having the correct gauge, length, and diameter.

Navel

The navel/belly button should be pierced with a 14g 7/16" curved barbell (sometimes called a banana bar). I do not recommend piercing the navel with a hoop. Hoops are prehistoric and any piercer who is still using them needs to catch up with the times. Barbell piercings heal much faster and the piercing is tender for a shorter amount of time because the bar lays flat against the body. Hoops stick out, and every time you move, the hoop moves too, which keeps the piercing sore for a longer period of time. Many people believe that it is easier to clean the piercing with a hoop in. My answer to this is the barbell is not difficult to clean. If the navel is pierced with a hoop, it is too easy to pierce too much skin. This will leave the customer no choice but to wear a 1/2" navel bar, for which there is a very limited choice of styles.

Occasionally a new piercing will have excessive swelling. If the piercing swells to the point that it is trying to swallow the top bead of the navel bar, then we recommend going to a hoop. The hoop allows for all the swelling the body wants to do. This is rare, but it does happen occasionally, and it is the only time I recommend putting a hoop in a new navel piercing.

We see girls in my stores who need to have their navels pierced for the second time because the first time they had it done the piercer did not pierce through enough skin and the piercing grew out. This is a huge problem with a lot of piercing shops. It is important to pierce enough skin on the initial piercing, which makes it harder for the body to reject the piercing. The general rule is the skin should take up most of the bar, leaving only a small amount of the bar for swelling.

Tip: It is best to wear loose, comfortable clothing around the navel while it is healing. Pants that fit below the belly button are preferred for this piercing. Women who wear pantyhose or pants over their new piercing will usually find that it takes longer for it to heal. With any new piercing that will be covered by clothes, it is important to wear clean clothing.

Tongue

The tongue should be pierced with a 14g 3/4″ straight barbell. The tongue needs the longer 3/4″ barbell because of the excessive swelling that follows the piercing. If a person has an unusually thick tongue, then a 7/8″ length bar should be used. As soon as the swelling is gone, which is usually one to two weeks but it varies with each person, it is essential to downsize to a shorter bar so you do not chip your teeth. (What to wear after the piercing is healed and tips for downsizing the bar are discussed in the chapters ahead.)

The tongue can be pierced with surgical steel, titanium, and polycarbonate. Pink titanium and polycarbonate work well to hide the piercing for those who are not supposed to have it, but want it anyway. The tongue should only be pierced vertically, through the center.

Tip: It is important to wait until the swelling is completely gone before changing tongue jewelry, in order to avoid problems.

Web—Under the Tongue

The web under the tongue can be pierced with an 18g 5/16″ hoop. This is an unusual piercing. I was skeptical that the web would not hold the jewelry because it is so thin, but it does. It is tricky getting the bead on the hoop, but it is worth it. A piercer with small hands will do better with this piercing.

Labret or Lip/Marilyn Monroe/Medusa (Lip Piercings)

The labret or lip, Marilyn Monroe, and Medusa should be pierced with a 16g 3/8″ flat back labret for girls and a 16g 3/8″ or a 14g 3/8″ flat back labret bar for guys. If the lip is unusually thick, then a 1/2″ length bar is needed. The labret is pierced with the longer 3/8″ bar to leave room for swelling and can be downsized to a shorter bar after three weeks. If the lip is pierced with a 3/8″ bar but has excessive swelling, as can sometimes happen, then a 1/2″ flat back labret bar needs to be put in until the swelling goes down. The bar should only be changed within the first three weeks if the swelling is so bad that the skin is trying to swallow the jewelry. If the lip swells to the point it is swallowing the flat back on the inside of the mouth, it needs to be pushed back out immediately. If the flat back is not pushed back out, the skin will heal over it and the person will need to see a doctor to have the jewelry surgically removed.

The labret or lip, Marilyn Monroe, and Medusa can be pierced with surgical steel, titanium, gold, Bioflex, and polycarbonate. The polycarbonate or Bioflex labret bar is gentle on the teeth and gums.

The labret can also be pierced with a surgical steel or titanium hoop. I recommend a 16g hoop for girls and either a 16g or 14g hoop for guys, whichever they prefer. I do not like using 18g hoops for this piercing because they do not always hold the bead tight. The diameter of the hoop varies depending on the size of the lip. For the initial piercing, the hoop needs to have extra room on it to allow for swelling. After three weeks, a hoop that fits snug can be put in.

Tip: It is important to wait three full weeks before changing lip jewelry, to avoid problems. After a couple of weeks, the lip piercing seems healed, but changing it too soon can make it swell again.

Nose

The nose can be pierced with an 18g or a 20g nose screw. The nose can also be pierced with an 18g or a 16g hoop. Piercing the nose with a 16g nose screw is not recommended because when the person goes to change their jewelry, the standard size for nose screws or nose bones is 18g or 20g. If the thinner jewelry is inserted into the 16g piercing, the top of the jewelry sinks into the hole. I have seen many people very unhappy about this when they are trying to change their jewelry. Unfortunately, many piercers use 16g nose screws to pierce with, so make sure to ask what gauge is going to be used. If you choose to be pierced with a 16g hoop, downsize to an 18g hoop before trying to wear a nose screw. This will allow the piercing to shrink to the appropriate size to wear a nose screw or nose bone.

The nose should *never* be pierced with a nose pin or a nose bone. A nose pin is a small, straight bar that has a bead or stone on top. It is all one piece, with a varying length of 1/2″, 5/8″, or 3/4″ and can be 20g, 18g, or 16g. After inserting the straight pin into the nose, the piercer bends it into the *L* shape. Sometimes the long end of the pin is left hanging out the nose or some piercers will cut the end of it off with wire cutters, leaving a sharp edge inside the nose. In order for the end of the nose pin to be cut off, they have to insert wire cutters into the nose. The reasoning behind this is that they "custom fit" the jewelry to the nose. All I can think of every time I see or hear this is how painful it must be to have someone bend a piece of metal jewelry that is in your newly pierced nose. This sort of technique is lazy and irresponsible. If a piercer truly wants to custom-fit the jewelry, he or she could use the tool made to bend nose pins into screws and bend the jewelry before he or she inserts it. If the piercer is inserting a straight nose pin because he or she is not able to insert a nose screw, then the piercer is in need of more training.

Some piercers are not confident piercing with nose screws and the nose bones seem easier for them to use. A nose bone looks like the nose pin except it is shorter with a small bulb on the end to hold it in a healed piercing. When the nose swells from the piercing, it swallows the nose bone on the inside of the nose, healing completely closed on the inside, so the piercing does not go all the way through. When this happens, the jewelry must be removed and the nose has to be repierced.

The nose can be pierced with surgical steel, hermetical gold, titanium, and 14 kt gold. The hermetical gold nose screw is particularly good for this piercing because it is nickel-free, hypoallergenic, and specially processed so it will not flake or peel. The nose should only be pierced with an 18g or 20g nose screw or a 16g or 18g hoop.

Tip: If the nose screw should come out and you cannot put it back in, the best thing to do is put a straight earring stud in the piercing. This will keep the piercing open until you can get into a piercing shop to have the jewelry reinserted, which can save you from having to be repierced.

Septum

The septum can be pierced with a hoop or a horseshoe; either a 16g or a 14g looks good. We have found that most girls prefer the 16g, and guys choose either a 16g or a 14g. The diameter will vary depending on the size of the person's nose, but a 5/16" or 3/8" generally works well, leaving a little room for swelling.

Eyebrow

The eyebrow is usually pierced with 16g jewelry. It can be pierced with a curved bar, hoop, or horseshoe. For girls, 5/16" length bars work great. Because guys tend to have thicker eyebrows, the 3/8" length works best. If a guy has thin eyebrows, a 5/16" bar should be used. With hoops, the eyebrow can be pierced with a 5/16" or 3/8" diameter, depending on how thick the eyebrow is.

The eyebrow should not be pierced with 18g jewelry or straight bars because they have a greater tendency to grow out. Piercing too little skin can also cause it to grow out, leaving a noticeable scar on the face.

The eyebrow can be pierced with surgical steel, titanium, or gold.

Occasionally I see people who wear 14g jewelry in their eyebrow piercings. While it is fine to wear 14g, it is not recommended because if you ever decide to take the jewelry out, the 14g will leave a larger scar on the face.

Nipple

The nipple should be pierced with a 14g hoop or horseshoe, or a 14g bar. The length of the bar can vary from 1/2", 5/8", or 3/4", depending on the size of the nipple. When getting pierced with a bar it is important to use a bar that is long enough that it leaves room for swelling. The diameter of the hoop can vary from 1/2" to 5/8", also depending on the size of the nipple. It is important not to pierce with a hoop that is smaller in diameter than a 1/2" because it can make the nipple elongate. The nipple needs plenty of room on the jewelry for swelling and healing in order to maintain its original size.

The nipple can be pierced with surgical steel, titanium, and gold. Most people choose the hoop because of the price, but being pierced with a bar is more comfortable. The bar also lays flatter under clothing and tends to heal faster.

Tip: If a person sleeps on their stomach, he or she should sleep on a towel during the first week because if the person rolls over onto their new piercing, it could cause the nipple piercing to bleed. This is completely normal; you just need to be aware of it. The nipple tends to be an easy piercing during the healing process. Because it's in an area of the body that is protected, most people find that there is very little discomfort during healing.

The following section is dedicated to earlobe and specialty ear piercings. You can get creative with the ears because every part of the ear can be pierced. With the ears, the size of the jewelry needs to fit the size of the person's ear.

Earlobes and Outer Cartilage

The earlobe can be pierced with hoops, ear-piercing studs, labret bars, and curved and straight barbells. Earlobes can be pierced with just about any size jewelry from an 18g up to an 8g. Piercing with anything larger than an 8g puts a lot of stress on the ear. After six weeks, the lobe can be stretched further if that is what the person wants. The most common gauge for outer cartilage is a 16g hoop, although occasionally guys will want a 14g hoop.

If the lobe or cartilage is pierced with a hoop, any diameter will work as long as room is left for swelling. Large diameter hoops are not recommended for the upper cartilage because it is too easy to hook into when you're brushing your hair plus the smaller hoops look better in the cartilage.

Which is better to be pierced with, a hoop or a stud? A hoop is easier to clean and allows more airflow through the ear piercing to help with healing. However, if the person is diligent in cleaning the piercing twice a day, not touching it with dirty hands, sleeping on clean sheets, and keeping their hair clean, he or she will do just as well with a stud.

Every part of the ear can be pierced with surgical steel, titanium, and gold. When we perform needle piercings on the conch, cartilage, and fossa, we offer the piercing stud. Many people prefer this and are surprised that we will insert a regular piercing stud instead of a standard piece of body jewelry. Many women prefer this option for conch piercings. We are the only body piercers I know who use this method.

Tip: If the cartilage is being pierced with a hoop, but a stud may be worn at some point, the piercing should not be too close to the curve of the outer ear, to leave room for a stud to be worn.

Tragus

This is a very popular piercing. The tragus should be pierced with either an 18g or a 16g hoop. Personally, I do not like piercing with 18g hoops because the hoop is so thin, it is easy for the bead to pop out of the hoop. The 16g hoop is more reliable because it is stronger. It is also possible to insert a labret bar in the piercing, using a reverse insertion technique, although most piercers are not familiar with this method.

The positioning of this piercing is important so that if the person wants to wear a stud, the back of the earring will not show. The diameter of the hoop is generally 5/16". In some cases, if the tragus is really small, a 1/4" hoop might work; if the tragus is large, a 3/8" hoop might work. The standard tends to be 5/16" for look and comfort. The positioning on this piercing is also very important so that the hoop lies neatly within the ear.

Anti-Tragus

The anti-tragus piercing can be done with a 16g hoop or a curved eyebrow bar. The length or diameter will vary depending on the shape of the ear. A 5/16" or 3/8" barbell or a 5/16" hoop works well. A spiral (twisted horseshoe) also works well for this piercing.

Conch

The conch can be pierced using a hoop or an ear-piercing stud (that is, a needle piercing using a piercing stud for the insertion jewelry). A 16g or a 14g hoop works well for this piercing. It is important to use a hoop that is the right diameter to fit comfortably around the ear, leaving a little room for swelling.

Rook

The rook can be pierced with a 16g 5/16" curved bar or an 18g or a 16g hoop. This part of the ear is very small so when using a hoop, a 1/4" or 5/16" works great.

Daith

The daith is most commonly pierced with an 18g or a 16g hoop, either a 1/4" or 5/16" diameter. The daith can be pierced on the top or bottom, and if the daith travels down into the ear, it can be pierced inside the ear as well. The daith has room for multiple piercings and looks great with two or three hoops in it. An 18g or a 16g curved barbell can also be placed in this piercing, but it looks better with a hoop. The triple forward helix piercing has become very popular. This is three piercings, done with small labret bars on the daith.

Fossa

The fossa piercing is initially done with a piercing needle, and an ear-piercing stud—surgical steel, titanium, or hermetical gold—is inserted. Because of the positioning of this piercing, a hoop will not work for the fossa.

Industrial

The Industrial is pierced with a 14g straight barbell that can range in length from 1 1/4" to 1 3/4", depending on the size of the ear. One of the vendors I buy body jewelry from has 16g industrial bars and these can be used as well. I prefer 5 mm beads on this bar, especially for girls, rather than the larger 6 mm bead. This is a big piercing and it is common for people to have problems with it while it is healing. We have found that it sometimes helps to remove the bar, put in 14g hoops (or 16g hoops if it was pierced with a 16g bar) until the piercings are healed, and then reinsert the bar.

The Industrial can be pierced with surgical steel, titanium, or a hermetical gold bar.

Tip: It is very important that there is plenty of room left on the industrial bar for swelling.

CHAPTER NINE

Quick-Reference Guide: Piercing Jewelry

Please note that this is a *guide* for jewelry used in body piercing. Actual length or diameter may vary slightly depending on the person's body. When it comes to gauges, the larger the number, the thinner the bar or hoop will be. The smaller the number, the thicker the bar or hoop will be.

Even though I list 18g hoops for ear piercings, I personally will not pierce with 18g jewelry, except for the web under the tongue. I do not like 18g captive-bead hoops for piercing because the metal is so thin that if it gets pulled on, it is easy for the hoop to be pulled away from the bead. If this happens, the bead could be lost and the hoop could fall out. A 16g hoop is strong enough to hold the bead in without having to worry about it getting pulled on.

There is a type of body-piercing hoop called an annealed hoop. These hoops have the bead secured on one side of the opening, so it will not come off. The hoop is bendable, so the piercer does not need tools to open or close it. If the piercer doesn't have strong hands, it is easy to pull on the new piercing when closing this type of hoop. I prefer the captive hoop (also called a captive-bead ring), using the opening and closing tools to close the hoop and insert the bead, which puts no stress on the new piercing.

NAVEL
14g 7/16" curved barbell
14g 1/2" curved barbell (in rare cases)

TONGUE
14g 3/4" straight barbell
14g 7/8" straight bar *only* for thicker-than-average tongues

TONGUE WEB
    18g 5/16″ hoop

LABRET OR LIP/MARILYN MONROE/MEDUSA
    16g 3/8″ labret bar for girls
    16g or 14g 3/8″ labret bar for guys (7/16″ or 1/2″ length bar for
        thick lips)
    16g or 14g hoops, diameter varies depending on size of lip (3/8″,
        7/16″, 1/2″)

NOSE
    18g or 20g nose screw or a captive hoop 18g or 16g

SEPTUM
    16g 5/16″ hoop or horseshoe for girls
    14g 5/16″, 3/8″, or 7/16″ hoop or horseshoe for guys

EYEBROW
    16g 5/16″ curved bar/hoop for girls
    16g 5/16″ or 16g 3/8″ curved bar/hoop for guys

NIPPLE
    14g 1/2″ hoop
    14g 5/8″ hoop for larger nipple
    14g 1/2″, 5/8″, or 3/4″ straight bar

EARLOBES
    Piercing studs (20g)
    18g–8g hoops, 5/16″ to 1/2″ diameter, depending on size of lobe

OUTER CARTILAGE
    16g or 14g captive hoops, 5/16″ to 3/8″ in diameter
    Piercing stud

TRAGUS
    16g 5/16″ hoop (1/4″ for small tragus, 3/8″ for large tragus)

ANTI-TRAGUS
    16g 5/16″ or 16g 3/8″ curved barbell

16g 5/16" hoop

Conch
   Piercing stud
   16g 1/2" or larger hoop
   14g 1/2" or larger hoop

Rook
   16g 1/4" or 16g 5/16" hoop
   16g 5/16" curved barbell

Daith
   16g 1/4" or 16g 5/16" hoop or curved barbell

Fossa
   Piercing stud

Industrial
   16g or 14g 1 1/4" to 1 3/4" straight barbell

Tip: It is important to check threaded beads (screw-on beads) every day to make sure the beads stay on tight. Because they screw on, they can also come unscrewed, which makes it possible to lose or swallow the beads.

Chapter Ten

Piercing Aftercare

Aftercare has always been one of my greatest concerns. I am very fortunate to have been trained in the use and importance of care solution, and I have always given care solution with each piercing. It is not sold separately; it is included. Too many people go in for a piercing and come out with no idea of how to take care of it. It is essential for piercers to explain the care procedure to the customer at the time of the piercing. Aftercare recommendations vary among piercers. Some piercers tell their customers to wash with antibacterial soap. Others sell care products separately or recommend sea salt.

How someone takes care of his or her new piercing is extremely important. The following information is what I recommend.

Try to never touch your piercing except for cleaning, but make sure your hands are clean if you need to. I only recommend one product for aftercare and that is the piercing solution we use. I have used it since I started body piercing in 2000, with tremendous success. I believe this to be the best care solution on the market. It was designed specifically for body piercings, and it really works well to help piercings heal safely and quickly. It is nonstaining and very soothing to new and irritated piercings, and it does not dry out the skin. It is simply called SAFE Piercing Care Solution.

The solution is applied twice a day, once in the morning and once at night. Simply dip a cotton-tipped swab in the solution and clean around both sides of the piercing. Clean off any crusty buildup and clean any part of the bar or hoop that is not through the piercing. *Never remove jewelry to clean a new piercing.* After cleaning, rotate the jewelry gently through the piercing a couple of times to work the solution into the piercing. This is a good time to check to make sure threaded (screw-on) beads are on tight.

If you get a crusty buildup on the jewelry or around the piercing during the day, use a cotton-tipped swab and water to remove the buildup. After a few weeks, you can stop using the piercing care solution and start washing your new piercing in the shower with regular soap and water. Do not overclean the new piercing, because that can cause irritation.

It is very important to continue to clean your piercing every day, with the piercing solution or with regular soap and water, for as long as you have your piercing.

While your piercing is healing, you should never move the jewelry in your piercing when it is dry. This will irritate the piercing, and if there is crusty buildup attached to the skin and jewelry, moving it could cause the piercing to bleed, prolonging the healing time. Only move the jewelry in your new piercing when it is wet from cleaning it.

There are many different opinions from body piercers on how to care for your new piercing. At my stores, we see firsthand that rubbing alcohol, over-the-counter ointments, and sea salt do not work well for cleaning or initiating healing for piercings. But everyone is different. In the rare case that someone is not able to use the piercing care solution, or if it is not available, my suggestion would be to gently wash the piercing twice a day with regular soap (*not* antibacterial soap) and water. Make sure to rinse the piercing really well to get all the soap out of the piercing. I personally prefer soaps that do not contain chemicals. Sappo Hill[4] has a great selection of soap that is good to use on new piercings if a care solution is not available. Their lavender soap is mild and not drying to the skin.

The Scoop on Care Products

- Hydrogen peroxide. This product is not effective in eradicating bacteria and may cause excessive drying. Hydrogen peroxide is used on surface wounds because it bubbles up and promotes the removal of the top layer of skin, which is recommended to help heal surface wounds. With a piercing, you do not want to remove the top layer of skin. The skin needs to heal itself, leaving a clear channel for the jewelry to sit in.

4   www.Sappohill.com.

- Rubbing alcohol. This product is not effective in eradicating bacteria and may cause excessive drying of the skin.
- Antibacterial soap. This soap kills the good bacteria with the bad. It is better to use regular soap that will not kill the good bacteria that the skin needs to stay healthy and promote healing.
- Bactine and Neosporin. These products were developed to heal surface cuts, not to heal piercings. These ointments are sticky, so any dust particle in the air is attracted to them. If the body jewelry moves through the piercing and there is dust on the ointment, it pushes the dust particles inside the clean piercing. These ointments also keep the piercing moist, which can prevent or prolong healing.
- Sea salt and salt products. A new piercing needs to be cared for in the same manner as an open wound. The piercing needs to heal from the inside out. I have never heard of a doctor prescribing salt to treat an open wound. Many body piercers recommend sea salt as an aftercare product. Sea salt is something you should put on your food, not on your skin; it is very drying to the skin. Too many times, we hear customers talk of using table salt or Epsom salt on their piercings. I have also heard body piercers recommend table salt. I would think that would burn on a new piercing. Have you ever heard that expression, "That's like putting salt in a wound?"
- Tea tree oil. I have had customers who swear by the healing effects of tea tree oil. I have to stick to my convictions that if the word "oil" is in the name of any product, it could be sticky or oily on the piercing, attracting dust particles. It could also keep the piercing moist, prolonging the healing process. Although tea tree oil has healing properties for other conditions, healing a piercing is not one of them.
- Medicated soaps made for piercings. These liquid, medicated soaps that are sometimes recommended by piercers kill the good bacteria along with the bad bacteria. These soaps can also be very drying to the skin.
- Regular soap. Regular soap (which is not antibacterial) is my second choice for cleaning a new piercing. A mild soap will work well, but it is important that all the soap be rinsed from the piercing site.

- SAFE Piercing Care Solution. This is a solution designed to help piercings heal properly. It is nonstaining, does not sting the new piercing, and is very soothing.
- Sweet Pea Piercing Solution. This solution, which contains natural enzymes, is an anti-inflammatory and is excellent for infection control. It is nonstinging, and nontoxic. We have been testing it specifically for use on piercings that are having problems and have had good results. Two of my piercers used it on piercings they were having problems with—one on an anti-tragus and one on a dermal anchor—neither of which wanted to heal. Both piercings were red, irritated, and sore. Both had very quick healing results with this solution. It works well to help irritated piercings heal quicker. Our customers love this product; the feedback has been very positive.

For oral piercings (tongue and lip), an antiseptic mouthwash should be used after smoking, eating, and drinking for two weeks after the piercing. Only rinse for six seconds. Many piercers do not recommend using an antiseptic mouthwash with alcohol, but we have found that as long as you do not over-rinse (no longer than six seconds), there are no issues. Additionally, the antiseptic mouthwash can be diluted up to 50 percent with water and antiseptic mouthwash without alcohol can also be used. Ice placed on the tongue will help with swelling.

I can only make recommendations based on my knowledge and experience. Ultimately, people will do whatever they feel most comfortable with, and we have to respect that, whether we agree with it or not. My stores have performed over eighty-six thousand piercings, and with every one of those piercings, we gave a bottle of piercing care solution, a bottle of mouthwash (tongue piercing), or both (lip piercings). We have seen amazing results with the piercing care solution, and it is still the only product I recommend to care for a new piercing.

Tip: Be gentle when cleaning your new piercing. Only clean the new piercing twice a day unless doing a physical activity that requires you to clean perspiration away from the piercing site. Overcleaning can cause irritation.

CHAPTER ELEVEN

When Can I Change My Body Jewelry?

It never ceases to amaze me how impatient people are to change their body jewelry. Even when they have just been pierced, most of them want to change their body jewelry the next week. It is worth waiting out the healing time so that you do not create a problem with the piercing. I have had many girls tell me they changed their jewelry after a week or two without any problems. They are lucky, because we see a lot more girls who changed their jewelry too soon and had major problems. I cannot state this enough: it is worth the wait! Even though the piercing looks healed on the outside, it is still healing on the inside. The following healing times apply to most people; but human bodies vary, and for some, healing can take longer.

Body-Piercing Healing Time
When it is okay to change jewelry

Navel—four to six months

Tongue—as soon as the swelling goes down. Everyone is different, but usually two weeks

Labret or Lip/Marilyn Monroe/Medusa—three weeks

Nose/Septum—six weeks

Eyebrow—four months

Nipple—four months

Lobe/Cartilage/Rook/Daith/Tragus/Conch/Fossa/Anti-Tragus/ Industrial—six weeks (for some, cartilage and industrial piercing may take longer than six weeks to heal)

Tip: When changing jewelry, wash your hands before you begin. Clean the piercing site and the jewelry before inserting it. For cleaning, use care solution for external piercings and an antiseptic mouthwash for tongue and lip piercings. Jewelry slides into the piercing easier if the piercing is wet, but make sure your hands are dry so you do not drop the jewelry.

CHAPTER TWELVE

Body Jewelry: After the Piercing Is Healed

A piece of jewelry that one person can wear may not work for another person because everyone's body is different. Part of wearing body jewelry is trial and error, but there are some standards that work well for most people. Remember, when it comes to gauges, the larger the number, the smaller (thinner) the bar or hoop will be.

As I mentioned above, part of wearing body jewelry is trial and error. This may mean purchasing jewelry to wear and then discovering that it doesn't fit the way you had hoped it would. Maybe you don't like how it looks once it is inserted into the piercing. Body jewelry should not be returned, because it cannot be resold, due to health concerns, so there is some financial investment involved in finding which jewelry is preferable to wear. Do your best to buy the correct gauge, length, and diameter.

We have many customers who are comfortable changing their own body jewelry, and others who prefer us to change it for them. Most piercing studios will change body jewelry, although sometimes there is a fee. Our policy is that there is no charge to change jewelry that was purchased from us; we do charge a small fee to change jewelry that the customer purchased elsewhere.

Some people need to hide their piercings for work or for other reasons. There are types of body jewelry called *retainers* that are made to hide the piercing. Retainers are a clear acrylic, Bioflex, Pyrex glass, or polycarbonate material and are made for the eyebrow, lip, nose, septum, navel, and tongue piercings.

When the piercing is healed and it is time to change the jewelry, it is good to have an understanding of the different types of body jewelry that are available. Longer jewelry is initially used for some piercings to allow for swelling, so it is important to know what length to downsize to after the piercing is healed and to understand the steps in the downsizing process.

The following list goes into detail about the different types of jewelry that can be worn in healed piercings. This information will be simplified into a quick-reference guide in the next chapter.

Navel

Standard size for navel jewelry is 14g 7/16". If a person is pierced too deep (too much skin was pierced), he or she may need to wear jewelry in a longer 1/2" length. If a person was pierced too shallow or if the piercing migrated (jewelry moved itself lower), he or she may need to wear a shorter bar in a 3/8" length. Banana barbells (curved barbells), hoops, spirals, and horseshoes can all be worn in the navel. There is a large variety of 14g navel jewelry to choose from. With long dangles, one needs to be careful about catching it on the top of pants or belts. Long dangles are best worn for special occasions. Shorter dangles generally work fine for everyday use.

If someone has an allergy to sterling silver, which contains nickel, some types of dangle jewelry should be avoided. If the bar above the dangle has two round stones (one on top and one on the bottom), and the metal around the stones is the same color as the surgical steel bar, then the whole bar and balls are surgical steel. If the stone on the bottom bead is not set in a completely round setting or is in a prong setting and the color appears shinier than the top bead and bar, it is probably rhodium plated or sterling silver. Acid in some people's system can wear the rhodium plating off, making the bar lose its shiny finish. Some people's skin may have a reaction to the rhodium or sterling silver. Unfortunately, some people do not know they cannot wear certain types of jewelry until they try it.

After the piercing is healed, it is okay to wear a hoop; just make sure the hoop is the correct diameter. If the hoop is too big around it will be uncomfortable and could easily get pulled, possibly tearing or irritating the piercing.

Tongue

Once the swelling goes down on the tongue, which usually takes about two weeks, a shorter bar should be inserted to prevent chipping teeth. The length to downsize to is 14g 5/8". This is the standard length for tongue bars, and this length works for most people. For some, this bar will still feel too long. After you try a 14g 5/8" bar, if you are still biting down on the beads, you need to go to the shorter 14g 1/2" bar. It is best to downsize one length at a time until you find the length that is the most comfortable.

When choosing your barbells, remember that if the beads are large, it will make the bar longer in your mouth than a bar with smaller beads. Flat top bars are great if you need to occasionally hide your piercing. You can flip the bar around to show the bead, or hide the piercing with the flat top. These come in acrylic, polycarbonate, surgical steel, and titanium.

Many people like the acrylic beads because they are easier on the teeth if you bite down on the jewelry. Acrylic jewelry in the mouth does not have a very long lifespan. When you eat or drink foods that are hot, it heats up the acrylic. If you eat or drink foods that are cold, it cools it down. The constant change in temperature on the plastic makes it brittle and eventually it will break. Alcohol and mouthwash also dries out the acrylic and makes it brittle. Plus, you have to be careful not to overtighten acrylic beads or you will strip the threads. A good fitting metal bar is always best.

TIP: If you are biting down on your beads, your bar is too long.

Web—Under the Tongue

The web under the tongue can be pierced with an 18g 5/16″ hoop. This is an unusual piercing. The jewelry for this piercing needs to be kept lightweight in order to discourage tearing and rejection. The bead must be very secure on the hoop to ensure it will not come off. Jewelry for this piercing does not need to be changed.

Labret/Lip

Three weeks after the piercing, a shorter, more comfortable labret bar can be put in. Both 16g and 14g labret bars work great for this piercing. When downsizing to a shorter bar, the downsize length may vary, depending on the size of the lip. The first length down is 5/16″ and this length works well for most people. For anyone with thin lips, the 5/16″ bar may still be too long and a 1/4″ bar may fit better, especially for Monroe piercings. It is best to downsize one length at a time until you find the length that works best.

Both 16g and 14g hoops can be worn, using any diameter that fits the lip, usually 5/16″, 3/8″, or 7/16″. The 16g micro-labret bars (with a tiny 2 mm bead or stone) for lip piercings on girls, are tiny and feminine.

Surgical steel, titanium, gold, and Bioflex bars can all be worn; the Bioflex bars are very comfortable and easy on the teeth and gums.

After the piercing is healed, a third option for jewelry is the fishtail labret. I have also seen girls use nose screws in their labret and Monroe piercings. I do not really recommend this, but it seems to work for some people.

TIP: For all lip piercings, downsize the bar in steps. From the 3/8" piercing bar, the first downsize length is 5/16". If the 5/16" is still too long, then go to the 1/4" length bar.

Marilyn Monroe/Medusa

A 16g 1/4" or 16g 5/16" labret bar works perfect for Monroe and Medusa piercings. The first downsize length should be 5/16", and then if that is still too long, go to a 1/4" length labret bar. The 16g micro-labret is adorable for these piercings. This is a labret bar with a 2 mm stone. It looks like a tiny sparkle above the lip.

The Bioflex bars are recommended for this type of piercing for comfort, and they are gentle on the teeth and gums, but surgical steel, titanium, and gold can also be worn. Jewelry can be changed after three weeks.

Nose

There is a huge variety of jewelry to choose from for the nose. What one person likes to wear, another may not like. One really has to try the different jewelry to see what works best for their nose. There are nose screws, nose bones, nose pins, and hoops. Some people are actually able to wear short nose pins (kept straight) comfortably without the pin falling out of their nose, but this does not work for most people.

The nose jewelry can be changed after six weeks, if desired. At that time, the jewelry can be changed to a different nose screw, hoop, nose bone, or small nose pin. The drawback for the nose bone is it has small beads on both ends. The bead going in is larger than the shaft of the jewelry so it can be uncomfortable inserting this type of jewelry. After it is inserted, the piercing heals down around the shaft of the jewelry, making it hard and sometimes impossible to remove. The top of the nose bone usually has to be cut off with a small pair of wire cutters to remove the jewelry. Nose bones come in sterling silver and surgical steel and they are fairly inexpensive. They work great for those who do not want to change their jewelry.

For someone who does not like wearing nose screws or nose bones, the small nose pin works well. It is a 20g pin, with a small stone or ball on top. It can be bent into an *L,* and then the end can be cut and filed smooth to make it a perfect fit before inserting it in the nose. They come in 14 kt gold, surgical steel, and sterling silver.

For people who like to wear a hoop in their nose but have trouble changing it, a great nose hoop is now available. It is easily inserted from the inside of the nose and it looks like a full hoop, even though it isn't. This nose hoop is available in 20g and 18g surgical steel, titanium, and gold PVD (physical vapor deposition, which is a gold plating) in 1/4", 5/16", and 3/8" diameters. No tools are required to insert or remove this hoop.

With a lot of nose jewelry, the stones are glued in, and they fall out easily from being worn in the shower. This is because the soap and water loosen the glue. I highly recommend nose jewelry that has prongs holding the stone or that has stones that are press-fit, which should keep you from constantly replacing the jewelry.

You generally do not see body jewelry made from sterling silver except for nose bones and pins. Sterling silver should only be worn in a completely healed piercing. There is more information about wearing sterling silver in a nose piercing in the FAQ section at the back of the book.

Septum

After six weeks, smaller jewelry or a retainer can be inserted into a septum piercing—or the initial piercing jewelry can be left in. The horseshoe jewelry can be flipped up inside the nose to hide the piercing. A 16g or 14g hoop or horseshoe with a small diameter of 5/16" or 3/8" looks really good in this piercing. There are also different types of septum jewelry available such as metal and organic spikes, septum mustache jewelry, and retainers.

Eyebrow

Both 16g and 18g are popular sizes for eyebrows, although I recommend staying with 16g jewelry for this piercing. Curved bars are best because straight bars tend to grow out easier. The length of the bar depends on how long the piercing is. Usually this will be 5/16" or 3/8". If not very much skin is pierced, or if the piercing migrates (top hole moves lower), a 1/4" bar could be put in. Hoops and horseshoes can also be worn in this piercing. It is better to keep the jewelry in this piercing small (16g) because when the jewelry is removed, it does leave scars. I never recommend 14g jewelry for the eyebrow because it leaves larger scars when the jewelry is removed, and because the 14g jewelry is sometimes too heavy for this piercing.

Nipple

There is a lot of great jewelry available for this piercing. Although 14g jewelry is standard, some people do stretch this piercing. This is not a piercing I recommend stretching because it is such a small area. There is not a lot of skin there, and you have to be really careful. Hoops (any diameter after the piercing is healed), straight or curved bars (tongue and navel bars work for the nipple), and horseshoes all fit for this piercing.

Nipple shields are also very popular and come in lots of fun styles. The key to buying nipple shields is to make sure the nipple will fit inside the shield (size and styles vary). The nipple is a little harder to clean with a shield on, so make sure to lather up the whole area, including jewelry and rotate the jewelry back and forth, then rinse well while in the shower.

Ears

I prefer a small gauge (16g) in the daith, rook, tragus, and cartilage. The lobes can be stretched as desired. My preference for cartilage piercings is 16g, except on the industrial and outer cartilage, which can go up to a 14g. Just about any size and type of jewelry can be worn in the ears as long as it is comfortable: hoops, horseshoes, straight and curved bars, plugs, and labret bars.

CHAPTER THIRTEEN

Quick-Reference Guide: Jewelry for Healed Piercings

P lease note that this is a guide for jewelry that can be worn in a healed piercing. This is what works well for most people, but the actual length or diameter may vary slightly depending on the person's body.

When it comes to the gauge, the larger the number, the smaller (thinner) the bar or hoop will be.

NAVEL
    14g 7/16" curved barbell (standard size)
    Deep navel piercings will need a 1/2" bar
    Shallow piercings will need a 3/8" bar

TONGUE
    14g 5/8" straight barbell (standard length)
    14g 1/2" for thinner tongues
    14g 3/8" for super thin tongues
    Clear acrylic retainers with beads or flat top with O-ring

WEB—UNDER THE TONGUE
    18g 5/16" hoop

LABRET OR LIP/MARILYN MONROE/MEDUSA
    Length of bar depends on thickness of lip
    16g 5/16" labret bar for girls (16g 1/4" for thinner lips)
    14g 3/8" or 14g 5/16" labret bar for guys
    16g or 14g hoops, diameter varies depending on size of lip
    Flat top retainer (clear) with O-ring or clear bead

Nose

18g or 20g nose screw, hoop, nose bone, or nose pin (bent into an *L*)

Retainer (flat top or round bead, clear)

Septum

16g 5/16" hoop or horseshoe for girls

14g 5/16", 3/8", or 7/16" hoop or horseshoe for guys

16g or 14g retainers that flip up into the nose to hide the piercing

Horseshoes can also be flipped up to hide the piercing

Metal or organic septum spikes

Eyebrow

16g 5/16" or 1/4" curved bar or hoop for girls

16g 5/16" or 16g 3/8" curved bar or hoop for guys

Nipple

14g 1/2" or 7/16" hoop

14g 5/8" hoop for larger nipple

14g 7/16", 1/2", or 5/8" (depending on size of the nipple) straight or curved bar

Earlobes

Piercing studs (20g)

18g to 8g hoops, any diameter (5/16" to 1/2"), depending on size of lobe

Lobes can be stretched to wear larger plugs

Outer Cartilage

16g or 14g hoops, 5/16" or 3/8" in diameter

Tragus

16g 5/16" hoop

16g 1/4" or 5/16" labret bar

Earring stud

Anti-Tragus

16g 5/16" or 16g 3/8" curved barbell

16g 5/16″ hoop

CONCH
Earring stud
16g 1/2″ or larger hoop
14g 1/2″ or larger hoop

ROOK
16g 1/4″ or 16g 5/16″ hoop
16g 5/16″ curved barbell

DAITH
16g 1/4″ or 16g 5/16″ hoop
16g 1/4″ or 5/16″ curved barbell
16g 1/4″ labret bar for forward helix

FOSSA
Earring stud

INDUSTRIAL
16g or 14g straight barbell, 1 1/4″ to 1 3/4″ length, depending on
length of piercing

CHAPTER FOURTEEN

How to Change Body Jewelry

After the healing time is up, just about everyone wants to change their body jewelry, but most people are nervous about it. There are a couple of secrets to changing jewelry that really make a difference. First of all, it is important to clean the jewelry and the piercing prior to removing the jewelry. The jewelry slides in and out easier if it is wet. We recommend using our piercing solution to clean the jewelry and the piercing site before removing the jewelry. Then wet both sides of the piercing with the solution before inserting the new jewelry.

If you try to change belly button jewelry before the navel is healed on the inside, the barbell will not always go through. The threading on the bar catches on the unhealed skin and it will not push through.

Tongue and lip jewelry is easy to change on your own. The tongue bar can be inserted from the top or bottom. The labret bar is inserted from inside the lip. It will be easier to hold on to the beads if your hands are dry. If you change your bar over a sink, be sure to plug the sink so if you drop a bead it will not go down the drain!

People love wearing captive hoops, but have a hard time changing them. It is a great idea to buy your own tools and learn how to change your hoops any time you desire. This is easier than going to a piercing shop every time you want to have your jewelry changed.

Tip: With any jewelry that has threaded beads, the beads need to be checked daily so they do not come loose and fall off. There are many manufacturers of body jewelry and the threading on their jewelry is different, so beads are not always interchangeable.

CHAPTER FIFTEEN

Piercing Care: After a Piercing Is Healed

Most people think that once their piercing has healed, they do not have to take care of it any longer. As mentioned before, after a few weeks you can stop using the piercing care solution and start washing your new piercing in the shower with regular soap and water. You will always need to wash your piercing when you bathe—if you don't, it will smell bad!

If you have stretched earlobes, after they have healed, it is a good idea to remove the plugs at least once or twice a week and clean the piercing and the jewelry. Make sure you plug the drain in your sink so you do not lose your jewelry or rubber O-rings down the drain. For all other piercings, you should not remove the jewelry for cleaning.

Wearing organic plugs (bone, horn, wood, and porous stones) in the ears will help with the smell. Organic jewelry is porous, so it breathes, but it still needs to be cleaned. Wash them with a mild soap (no chemicals). Olive oil can be rubbed on wood plugs to keep them from cracking and keep them looking good. Olive oil is a good choice because it does not spoil like other oils do. Tea tree oil can be used to clean organic jewelry, but it can dry it out and cause it to crack. Organic jewelry should only be worn in healed piercings.

Tip: After the piercing is healed, and for as long as a person has a piercing, it should be washed daily in the shower with soap and water. Lather up the piercing, rotate the jewelry, and rinse well to remove all soap from the piercing.

CHAPTER SIXTEEN

Tapering

Tapering is stretching a piercing larger than its original size. The taper looks similar to a piercing needle except that it is not sharp on the small pointed end. Tapers come in every gauge size from 18g to 2". The large end of the taper is the gauge size and the narrow end generally tapers down to approximately two sizes smaller than its gauge size, for easy insertion into the ear.

Stretching should be done in stages so that the skin does not tear. Ears are the most popular piercing that people stretch. Care for a newly stretched piercing is the same as a new piercing: it should be cleaned twice daily with piercing solution. It is important to wait six weeks in between each stretch to allow time for proper healing.

The following steps are recommended for proper tapering of ears:

- Most people start out at 20g, 18g, or 16g. From these gauges, the first stretch can safely be made to a 10g.
- 10g to 6g is the next stretch. *After 6g, the ear should be stretched only one gauge at a time.* If you stretch larger than one gauge at a time going larger than 6g, you risk tearing the ear.

It is important to note, that even with stretching only one gauge at a time, it is possible for the ear to tear.

People tend to get in a hurry when they start tapering. Instead of taking it in steps, they want to jump to the larger size immediately. Take it slow; treat it as a new piercing. Let it heal, and then continue. Be patient, it is worth it!

While I recommend having ears tapered by a professional, many people choose to do this on their own. Piercing shops and retail body jewelry stores sell acrylic and steel tapers (also called expanders), for those who choose to stretch their own ears. These tapers come with an O-ring on it,

| 73 |

so the customer can insert and leave the taper in the ear, then slowly, over time, continue to push the taper further through to stretch the lobe.

There are different types of plugs that can be put in a gauged (tapered) ear. The easiest to insert is a single-flare plug or tunnel, as the back of the plug is the same gauge as the desired stretch. The other type of plug is a double-flared plug, which is flared out larger on each end. When buying plugs, it is important to consider that the gauge of a plug is measured at the middle point—the part that sits in the ear—not at the flare on the end.

I get asked all the time if stretched ears will heal back to normal. It depends on how big they are stretched and for how long. Obviously once the ears are stretched pretty large, the body cannot heal itself back to the original lobe size, but I have seen 0g tapering heal back to its original size. A lot also depends on how well the individual's body heals.

If the earlobes are stretched to a point where they will not heal back to their original size, surgery to correct the size of the lobes is an option. Dermatologist Wm. Phillip Werschler[5] works with patients to repair stretched and torn earlobes. In the process of repairing an earlobe that has been stretched, Dr. Werschler recreates the lobe by removing redundant tissue from the area. In recreating the lobe, he makes an attempt to match the original shape of the natural lobe. If this is not possible because of the extent of lost or damaged tissue, then he will typically create a pixie lobe, by sewing the lobe down to the side of the face instead of recreating a hanging lobe. If necessary, he will put a filler in the lobe during this process. Earlobes tend to be very forgiving in this situation.

In the case where there is only scar tissue in the lobe that needs to be removed, dermatologists are able to punch the scar tissue out of the ear with a special tool. A small amount of scar tissue will grow back, but the ears can be repierced.

Stretching ears has become very popular, and the selection of jewelry for stretched or gauged ears continues to evolve. The choices available for plugs, the most popular jewelry worn in stretched ears, includes surgical steel, titanium, gold plated, Pyrex glass, acrylic, glass, and organic material such as wood, bone, horn, and natural stone.

Tip: It is best not to stretch with double-flared plugs because you have to stretch up two sizes to get the plug in because of the flare. Stretching with

5   Wm. Phillip Werschler, MD/FAAD/FAACS, Personal Interview, 17 Nov. 2008, Assistant Clinical Professor of Medicine/Dermatology, University of Washington, Seattle and Spokane Dermatology Clinic, Spokane, WA.

single-flare plugs or tunnels is recommended. There are double-flared plugs on the market that screw together in the center, so you can taper with the correct gauge, but have the advantage of wearing a double flare. Plugs are measured at the middle point that sits in the ear.

Chapter Seventeen

Surface Piercings

As a matter of preference, I will not do surface piercings, even though we get many requests for them. I do not like the idea of performing surface piercings that will grow out and leave scars, and I have never seen a surface piercing that held for longer than a few months. I have changed jewelry for people who have gotten surface piercings whose bodies have started to reject the piercing, and they come to me to help them try to save it. We have tried different types of jewelry, but the body always wants to reject it.

I attended a class on surface piercings taught by the Association of Professional Piercers[6] and learned that in order for a surface piercing to have a better chance of not growing out, the placement of the jewelry needs to be deeper into the tissue. This is a very tricky procedure and requires the piercing be performed using the scooping method. The problems that can come from this type of procedure are a longer healing time and an increased risk of infection. I personally feel it is too much stress on the body to insert jewelry that deep under the skin.

Some piercers doing surface piercings use a hollow, flexible, plastic bar made from PTFE (Polytetrafluoroethylene). As I mentioned earlier, Teflon is one the trademarked names for PTFE. Ammonium perfluorooctanoate, one of the chemicals used in the production of Teflon, known as C-8, has been linked to cancer, organ damage, and other health risks in tests on laboratory animals.[7] Those chemicals could be absorbed directly through the skin, which is why I will not recommend that PTFE be inserted into the body. There are a couple of problems that come with using this type of bar. First, because it is hollow, blood from the piercing can back up into the bar, causing bacteria to grow and possibly resulting in an infection. In

---

6   Association of Professional Piercers, safepiercing.org.

7   "Teflon," (2 Dec. 2008): http://www.tuberose.com//Teflon.html.

order to avoid this, the bar needs to be changed during the healing period, causing more stress to the unhealed piercing.

If a surgical steel, staple-shaped, surface bar is used, as is more commonly seen; the ends of the bar, which are at a 45-degree angle, must be manipulated under the skin, through the tissue, causing additional stress to the area. This is especially difficult if the piercing being performed is a deeper surface piercing.

There is a dispute among body piercers on which is the best type of jewelry to use for surface piercings, the PTFE or the staple-shaped surface bar, to give this piercing a better chance of staying in. Unfortunately, there is no perfect jewelry to use for this type of body piercing.

I recently talked with a piercer who is having success using a surface bar with a 3/16″ rise on the 45-degree angle. With new jewelry continually being designed, I am hopeful that the success for this type of piercing will increase.

CHAPTER EIGHTEEN

Dermal Anchors

A dermal anchor, also known as a dermal or microdermal anchor, is a single-point piercing that gives the appearance of a single jewel, spike, or bead on the surface of the skin. This relatively new procedure has only been done since about 2008. The procedure is still being perfected, but with good results, and it is a great alternative to surface piercing. This type of piercing has an entrance point but not an exit. The base or foot of the anchor is inserted just beneath the skin and during the healing process, the tissue attaches to the base. Anchors are made from Grade 23 titanium and are internally threaded.

Microdermal anchors can be inserted using either a piercing needle or dermal punch. We prefer the piercing needle technique. Not all states allow this type of piercing, and some states do not allow the use of a dermal punch.

Microdermal anchors are manufactured in the size of 1/4" x 1/16", which is incredibly small. They can be placed anywhere on the body that has a flat surface of approximately three-quarters of an inch in diameter. Dermal anchors should not be placed on the hands, wrists, feet, or any flex points, because they do not heal well in those areas of the body.

Dermal anchors are available with a 16g or 14g rise that protrudes out through the skin to which a bead is attached. While the anchor remains in place, the beads can be changed (using a special tool to hold the anchor in place while changing the bead), to give a different look. Two types of dermal anchors are available, one with a solid foot for temporary placement and one with two hollow openings (a heel and toe on the foot) for long-term placement. The anchor with hollow heel and toe allows the tissue to attach for long-term placement.

As with any piercing, there is a chance that the anchor may grow out. Dermal anchors may become more popular than surface piercing, as it achieves the same visual effect, but the body will more easily accept this piercing.

When the time comes to remove the anchor, this procedure must be done by a piercer who is experienced in insertion and removal of dermal anchors. Because this type of jewelry is inserted beneath the skin, when it is removed, there is a chance of scarring.

As this is a type of piercing where the jewelry cannot be removed without the assistance of a body piercer, we will not do these on minors.

Microdermal anchors that are made from medical grade titanium are MRI safe, so one can leave it in for an MRI.

Medical Grade Titanium

Titanium 6AL4V and 6AL4V ELI, alloys made of 6% Aluminum and 4% Vanadium, are the most common types of titanium used in medicine. Because of its harmonizing factor with the human body, these titanium alloys are popularly used in medical procedures, as well as in body piercings. Also known as Gr. 5 and Gr. 23, these are some of the most familiar and readily available types of titanium in the US, with a number of distributors specializing in these specific grades.

Another benefit to titanium for use in medicine is its non-ferromagnetic property, which allows patients with titanium implants to be safely examined with MRIs and NMRIs.[8]

Aftercare for the dermal anchor should be followed precisely. A round band-aid should be placed over the dermal anchor for the first forty-eight hours, to ensure that it does not get pulled on and to encourage the initiation of the healing process. This piercing should be cleaned twice a day and a new/clean band-aid should be applied after each cleaning.

The healing time for dermal anchors is two to four months, and the bead can be changed after two months, if desired.

Swelling is not an issue with this type of piercing. The jewelry moves with the body if it swells, so the skin will not swell or heal over the piercing.

I have recently seen companies selling dermal anchors made from surgical steel. Because some surgical steels are magnetic, the jewelry could be pulled out by an MRI. This is why jewelry that is being set under the skin should only be medical grade titanium. Inserting a microdermal made

---

8   "Titanium: The Medical Metal of Choice," http://www.supraalloys.com/medical-titanium.php.

from surgical steel also opens the door to rejection if the person receiving the piercing has a nickel allergy.

There are people who would argue that this type of piercing is an implant. An implant is exactly what it sounds like: a foreign object is implanted and sealed under the skin, with no jewelry protruding through the skin as a piercing does. A dermal-anchor piercing is different in that it has the rise protruding through the skin, where the bead is attached, creating an exit point.

A dermal diver is a very new type of surface anchor. This jewelry is being manufactured in Germany and has recently become available in the United States. This is the smallest type of surface anchor available. Made from titanium, the shaft is only 1.2 mm thick and the shortest length is 1.2 mm. Dermal divers are inserted using a dermal punch.

What You Need to Know about Microdermal Anchors

The base of the anchor is called the foot. The foot has three parts to it: the smaller back of the foot is the heel, the longer front of the foot is called the toe, and the part that protrudes up through the skin is called the rise.

There are anchors that have holes in the foot and anchors that have a solid foot. The anchors with the solid foot are for customers who do not want the anchor to be permanent. The solid foot allows for easier removal. Anchors with holes in the heel and toe of the foot are for dermals that are meant to be permanent. As the piercing heals, the tissue attaches to the foot around the holes, anchoring it in.

Microdermal anchors absolutely should not be placed on hands, feet, wrists, on a bone (such as a collarbone) that is not flat, or on a joint or flex point. The dermals will not heal in these areas.

In order for a dermal to be successful, you need a flat area of skin, approximately one inch in diameter—about the size of a quarter.

Microdermal-anchor piercings should not be done on minors.

Medical grade titanium microdermal anchors are MRI safe— they do not have to be removed for an MRI because of its non-ferromagnetic property.

This is a single point piercing, not an implant.

Swelling is not an issue with this type of piercing. The jewelry moves with the body, so the skin will not swell or heal over the piercing site.

Removal of the dermal anchor could cause scarring, so choose the area of placement carefully.

CHAPTER NINETEEN

Female Genital Piercings

Women seek out genital piercings for personal and sexual expression. People are very curious about genital piercings, and I get asked if it is weird or uncomfortable doing this piercing. Speaking from experience, every piercing, no matter where it is located, is approached professionally. Concentrating on the area of the body being pierced should be foremost in the piercer's mind: Are there veins, moles, or freckles? Is there enough skin to pierce? These and a myriad of other factors figure into the area being pierced.

Especially with genital piercings, the body piercer should be keenly aware of the need to make the customer feel comfortable during the procedure.

A large number of female genital piercings are being done with 10g, 12g, and 14g jewelry. It is not necessary to use such a large gauge for this area. A 16g hoop or curved barbell would be better for comfort and healing, unless the woman specifically requests larger and heavier jewelry. As with other body piercings, we see ladies who were given no choice in jewelry for this piercing.

Loose clothing should be worn during the healing process in order to avoid the jewelry being tugged on, which can cause irritation and prolong the healing time. Loose clothing will also allow more airflow to help with healing. It is important to wear undergarments that are in good condition, and avoid lacy or frayed underwear, because if the jewelry catches on the underwear, it could damage the piercing or even tear out the jewelry.

When 14 kt gold jewelry is worn in genital piercings, it tends to tarnish faster due to exposure to urine. Gold jewelry needs to be cleaned (dipped) in a gold jewelry cleaner to retain its natural color.

Dr. Werschler points out that infection in genital piercings is more prevalent than other piercings, due to naturally greater levels of microflora (yeast, bacteria, fungi) in these areas, as well as varying levels of hygiene.

Infections usually come from natural bacteria in the area and poor hygiene after the area is pierced.[9]

The care for this type of piercing is the same as any other. The piercing should be cleaned twice a day with a piercing care solution or mild soap and water, rinsing well. One needs to be more aware of hygiene in this area in order to avoid problems.

Can sensation be lost from getting a genital piercing? Advanced Registered Nurse Practitioner Karen Kuehn says she has never heard of this happening and that as far as the piercing goes, it is quite safe. However, the damage most commonly caused from genital piercings is on females who use the jewelry to overstimulate themselves, causing damage to the area. Damage to female genitalia can also be caused from male genital piercings, and this type of damage leaves the female more susceptible to catching diseases.[10] With this type of piercing, care needs to be taken and one needs to be responsible and respect the other person's body.

A publication from Women's Health Queensland Wide points out that genital piercings could affect safe-sex practices by tearing or puncturing a condom.[11] To help avoid some of these problems, it is recommended to wear jewelry that does not have sharp edges and use a looser-fitting condom or use double condoms.[12]

It is advantageous for women to find a health-care practitioner who is caring and nonjudgmental about body piercing. As I have learned from Karen Kuehn, it is great to have a health care practitioner who is genuinely caring and concerned about women and their piercings, and being able to discuss piercings without being judged or feeling self-conscious is liberating. To our advantage, more nurse practitioners are becoming advocates for their patients who have piercings.

In an article written by Cathy Young and Myrna L. Armstrong, regarding nurses who care for patients with genital piercings, they said, "When a nurse acknowledges a woman's piercing and discusses it with her, she demonstrates that she is accepting and caring."[13] Nurses who receive

---

9   Werschler, Personal Interview.

10   Karen Kuehn, MSN, ARNP, Personal Interview, 05 Jan. 2006, Valley Obstetrics & Gynecology PS, Spokane Valley, WA.

11   http://www.womhealth.org.au.

12   http://www.aafp.org/afp/2005/1115/p2029.html.

13   Cathy Young, DNSc, APRN, BC, and Myrna L. Armstrong, EdD, RN, FAAN, "What Nurses Need to Know When Caring for Women with Genital Piercings,"

training in this area and are receptive to it are beneficial to women who have genital piercings.

Genital piercings are not recommended for anyone under eighteen, and any reputable piercer will refuse to perform this piercing on a minor. Minors should never have this area of the body pierced due to the anatomical changes that occur during adolescence.

I highly recommend only going to a piercer who is experienced in female genital piercings. There are many factors to be considered when doing these piercings, and if a piercer does not have the knowledge or experience needed, the piercing could lead to serious problems.

The most common types of female genital piercings are the VCH (vertical clitoral hood), HCH (horizontal clitoral hood), and outer labia, with the VCH being the most requested.

Not every woman has the anatomy for a VCH piercing, and it is up to the body piercer to determine if the anatomy is correct for the placement of this piercing. Generally, a 16g 3/8″ curved barbell is suitable for this piercing. A 16g hoop could also be used, but we have found that most customers prefer the curved bar for esthetics and comfort. The healing time is four weeks.

With HCH piercings, the piercer again must be sure that the anatomy is suited for this piercing. Because of the placement of the HCH, it must be done correctly in order to avoid piercing the clitoris. A 16g 3/8″ hoop is standard for this piercing. Healing time is four weeks.

The outer labia piercing can be done on any part of the outer labia and a 16g hoop or curved barbell is used for this piercing. The length or diameter of the jewelry depends on the build of the person, but it is generally 7/16″, because the jewelry needs to have sufficient room for swelling. The healing time is two to three months.

It is normal for this type of piercing to bleed in the beginning of the healing process. Urine is likely to sting during the first few days, but because urine is antiseptic, it will not cause problems. An increase in water intake will dilute the urine, lowering acidity.

Sexual activity is not prohibited during the healing process, but it must be gentle and hygienic. For your health and safety, use condoms for all sexual contact while the piercing is healing to prevent sharing bodily fluids, even if you are in a monogamous relationship.

Nursing for Women's Health (April/May2008): 129–37.

Tip: In order to qualify for genital piercings, a woman's body must be anatomically suited for these piercings; it is of the upmost importance to seek out a body piercer who has been properly trained to do female genital piercings.

CHAPTER TWENTY

Male Genital Piercings

We get a lot of requests for male genital piercings, and even though I have had some training, we do not perform them. Because I have limited experience in this area, I feel it is best not to comment on which jewelry is best to pierce with, care, etc. for these piercings.

What I find interesting is that we get requests for these piercings from all age groups of men from those in their twenties to men in their fifties and sixties. The most common of the male genital piercing and the one that people are most familiar with is the Prince Albert, which is also referred to as a PA.

Male genital piercing is done using captive bead hoops, horseshoe jewelry, and barbells. The piercing can be done through the skin on the shaft of the penis, the head of the penis, through the foreskin and the scrotum. It should be noted that piercing straight through the shaft of the penis could cause serious damage and should be avoided.

For anyone who is considering a male genital piercing, seek out a piercing professional who has proper training and experience.

CHAPTER TWENTY-ONE

Infection Control

Even a healed piercing can become infected. Most infections start from touching the piercing with dirty hands, not cleaning it properly, or playing with the jewelry too often—leave it alone until it is healed! If the jewelry accidentally gets pulled on, that can also start irritation to the piercing site.

If an infection starts within forty-eight to seventy-two hours after being pierced, the infection could possibly have come from the actual piercing, and if the infection starts after seventy-two hours of being pierced, the client most likely caused the infection by coming into contact with an irritant or touching the area with dirty hands. Surgical axiom indicates that infections in the first forty-eight to seventy-two hours are related to the procedure and after that from post-procedure wound care, mostly not washing hands. Infections come from natural bacteria in the area and hygiene after the piercing.[14]

How do you know if your piercing is infected? The online journal *American Family Physician* states, "If your piercing is infected, the skin around the area may be red and swollen. It might hurt to touch your piercing, and there may be a yellowish, bad-smelling fluid coming from the hole."[15]

In my experience dealing with people who have come into my stores with infections (whether I pierced them or not), I have never seen an infection that started with the initial piercing. The best thing someone can do to avoid infection is not to touch the piercing, and if you have to touch it, wash your hands first.

Many people believe their new piercing is infected during the healing process. They think that if their piercing is red or sore or oozing that it is infected. It is normal for a new piercing to be red and look irritated while it is healing. It is also normal for new piercings to ooze a clear or milky-colored substance while healing. It is not normal for the piercing to ooze a green or yellow substance.

---

14   Werschler, Personal Interview.

15   http://www.aafp.org/afp/2005/1115/p2035.html.

Only a licensed medical doctor can diagnose an infection. If you need to see a doctor because your piercing may be infected, try to find a doctor who is not opposed to body piercing. Many times I have had people tell me that they went to the doctor and their piercing was diagnosed as infected. The doctor told them to remove the jewelry and put them on antibiotics. In most cases, jewelry should be left in an infected piercing so that the piercing can drain. Removing the jewelry will heal the infection inside the piercing. Not all doctors are trained to know what to do in situations dealing with body jewelry and piercings. Try to locate a doctor who knows how to properly treat problems with piercings.

Occasionally we have customers who need to cover their piercing in order to play sports. We always recommend finishing the season before getting a new piercing, but once in a while we are asked the question, "Can I just cover my piercing and seal it with tape?" If you have covered the piercing and are sweating from an activity, the bacteria in your perspiration will build up around your new piercing and be trapped in a moist environment, which is perfect for growing bacteria. It is very important that the covering is removed as soon as possible and that the piercing is properly cleaned so that it does not get infected.

What should you do if you suspect the piercing is infected? First, make sure you follow the proper care and cleaning of the area as recommended by the piercing professional.

We have found that the following regime works well. Clean the piercing and jewelry (do not remove jewelry from piercing) twice a day (morning and night) with a mild soap, rinsing well, and then apply a product made specifically for infection control, such as Sweet Pea Piercing Solution. Gently rotate the jewelry to work the solution into the piercing.

Dr. Werschler advises patients to, "first follow the recommendation of the piercing professional, and if that does not resolve the concern, obtain an over-the-counter, topical antibiotic (such as Triple Antibiotic Ointment) that can be tried for a few days." Generally, in the case of a mild infection, the jewelry can be left in the piercing, which may help the infection to drain. The exception to this depends on the severity of infection. Mild infections can usually be managed with antibiotics and wound care, as described above. More serious infections (impetigo, cellulitis, sinus tracts, etc.) need prompt medical attention and may need to have the area cleared of any foreign bodies (such as jewelry) to heal properly.[16]

---

16   Werschler, Personal Interview.

Tip: Touching the piercing with dirty hands, wearing dirty clothes over the piercing, sleeping on bed sheets that are not clean, piercings being tugged on, being licked by pets, not rinsing soap or shampoo completely away from the piercing site, or not bathing frequently can cause irritation and possibly infection to the piercing.

Hypertrophic Scars and Keloids

Sometimes a piercing will develop what looks like a bubble. Although we usually call it a bubble, it is actually a cyst, which can be either infectious or noninfectious (granulomatous). It is also common for the cyst to be called a keloid, but this is not accurate.

Just like acne, simply draining the cyst can speed healing. If draining it doesn't resolve the problem, or if it worsens, then medical attention should be sought.[17] To get rid of the bubble, it needs to be drained twice a day. If it is not allowed to drain, the cyst can harden into a hypertrophic scar. The hypertrophic scar, once it hardens, will never go away, so it is important to do this as soon as it shows up. Sometimes this happens because the body is having a reaction to the jewelry and simply changing from surgical steel to titanium can solve the problem. A piercing can also get a bubble on it if it gets pulled on or if a foreign substance gets into the piercing.

In an article from the online resource of A Board Certified Plastic Surgeon, the following is written about hypertrophic scars and keloids:

> Hypertrophic scars appear as thick, red scarring due to an injury or other damage to the skin. These types of scars are sometimes confused with keloid scars because both types are similar in shape and size. Keloid scars tend to grow outside of the immediately affected area, however. Hypertrophic scars usually restrain their size and growth to only the immediate affected area.
>
> Hypertrophic scars also tend to heal themselves, decreasing in size and irritability over time, usually a twelve- to eighteen-month period. The scars will not disappear entirely, however.
>
> Hypertrophic scars are similar to keloid scarring in that they share a commonality in casualty. Both occur due to surgery, injections, body piercing, acne, or some trauma to the skin. Both types of scars can also be caused by skin surgery, or other restorative surgical procedures involving the skin.

---

17   Ibid.

Unlike keloid scarring, there seems to be no relationship to ethnic or family history associated with hypertrophic scars. Collagen levels in both keloid and hypertrophic appear to be similar in bulk, much more than in normal scar tissue. Hypertrophic scars are most likely to appear on the breastbone, ears, and shoulder, but may occur anywhere on the body.

In terms of healing, hypertrophic scars tend to heal themselves, decreasing in pain and swelling over a period of time (usually about a year or more). The healing process may be aided and hastened with the help of steroid topical ointments or steroid injections. Further steroid injections will help the scar recover faster.

Hypertrophic scar revision and surgery utilizing a type of excision or atraumatic closure with a reorientation using Z-plasty or the like often produces quick and detectable results. This surgical excision is the most prescribed method of surgically aiding hypertrophic scarring. Further hypertrophic scarring may occur, however, as a side effect of the surgery.[18]

Fibroplasia is the formation of fibrous tissue and is a normal healing response in the healing of wounds. Keloids and hypertrophic scars are abnormal healing responses. Hypertrophic scars and keloids are both benign. Cortisone injections can also be used to treat hypertrophic scars, and although it does not remove the scar, it will soften it.[19]

As mentioned in a previous chapter, I have found that Sweet Pea Solution works well on irritated piercings. PCMX and Southside Sea Solution are also great products, but have gone off the market; I feel they are worth mentioning in the event they resurface.

---

18   www.aboardcertifiedplasticsurgeonresource.com/scar-revision/hypertrophic-scars.html.

19   Werschler, Personal Interview.

CHAPTER TWENTY-TWO

Multiple Piercings in One Area

Just about every part of the ear can be pierced. Forget the old wives' tale about paralyzing your face by having cartilage pierced. It is crazy that some people still believe that. The ears provide an area for the most interesting piercings you can come up with. It is an open canvas.

The navel can be pierced all the way around it, on the top, bottom, and both sides. Some girls have gotten really creative with their belly-button jewelry and multiple piercings. We suggest doing only two piercings in the navel at a time and waiting before adding more piercings to allow for proper healing.

The tongue can be pierced more than once if it is long enough. If a person wants to have multiple tongue piercings, it is important to start the first one as far back as possible to allow room for the second or third piercing. When someone gets a second tongue piercing, it is important to put the 3/4" bar back into the first piercing to allow room for swelling.

The lip also has room for multiple piercings, and I have seen some creative labret piercings that look great. Two at a time is also a good limit for lip piercings, to allow for proper healing and not put too much stress on the area.

The nipple can be pierced horizontally, diagonally, or at a slant. Multiple nipple piercings can be done, but one has to take care with that area of the body. Having multiple piercings through the nipple would depend on the size of the nipple. If the piercings are not done correctly and are too close together, the piercings could grow into each other, creating one big piercing.

The nose also has room for multiple piercings and looks good with two or three. It is important that the piercings are spaced properly to allow room for the jewelry on the inside of the nose; otherwise, it could be uncomfortable.

The eyebrow can also have multiple piercings. They should be spaced far enough apart that the piercings do not grow into each other, creating one big piercing and possibly leaving a large scar.

CHAPTER TWENTY-THREE

Why Do People Pass Out?

It is important to eat a meal about a half an hour before getting pierced. Getting pierced is a big adrenaline rush. When the piercing is over and the body starts to relax, the blood sugar level can drop, making someone feel light-headed. If the person does not have enough nutrients in the body to hold their blood sugar level, he or she can get light-headed or pass out. We find that most people who pass out have skipped one or two meals before coming in to get pierced. We keep juice pouches on hand to get their blood sugar back up so they feel good again.

For some, if they have skipped two or more meals, they may have to eat some carbohydrates along with the juice to make them feel good enough to stand up and walk. For someone who is nervous about getting a piercing, eating a big meal directly before the piercing can cause them to feel nauseated. The food needs to digest a little first. I have had several people tell me that when they were pierced at tattoo studios, they were sent on their way immediately after the piercing. By the time they got to the parking lot, they passed out. We always give care instructions after the piercing so we can watch the customer for a few minutes to make sure they are okay. We watch their eyes to see if he or she stops focusing, and we watch the color in their face and lips so we know if they are going to pass out. Before someone passes out, their eyes can stop focusing and their face and lips go pale. There have been occasions where we have had customers pass out before they even get pierced. People can get their bodies so stressed out that they make themselves pass out.

Anyone who gets really worked up about the piercing should be monitored closely afterward. If you are prone to passing out after getting pierced, you should let your piercer know this.

Occasionally we have friends or moms of the person we are piercing pass out just from watching the piercing. We have had customers who wet their pants and worse. It is very embarrassing for them, and we act as though we don't notice, and we try to handle the situation as professionally as possible.

Once in a while, we get someone who will throw up after the piercing. We keep a small trash can handy for this event. I had a guy come in to get his nipples pierced, and after I pierced his first nipple, he threw up. He pulled himself back together, and then I pierced his other nipple. It is all in a day's work.

If you are in a situation where you are getting pierced or having jewelry changed and start to feel light-headed or nauseous, tell your piercer immediately. It's good for the piercer to have some warning before these things happen. It is for the safety of the person getting pierced, and it helps the piercer to be prepared.

CHAPTER TWENTY-FOUR

Frequently Asked Questions

1. *My jewelry came out and I can't get it back in.* No matter how many times we tell someone to check their beads every day, twice a day, it still happens that he or she loses a bead and their bar comes out. If the piercing is still fairly new, it can start to heal up immediately. If the jewelry will not go back in on its own, a body piercer can sometimes use a taper to help reinsert the jewelry.

2. *My navel piercing seems healed; can I change my jewelry?* We see a lot of girls who try to change their jewelry too soon. They remove their piercing jewelry then cannot get it back in because the piercing is not healed. Sometimes a hoop will have to be inserted if the threaded jewelry will not go through. Threaded jewelry goes through healed piercings just fine, but if the skin inside the piercing is not healed, the threads on the bar catch on the unhealed skin and it will not push through. It is worth the wait to let it heal. If the 14g bar will not go in (either because it is not healed enough or because the piercing has started to heal closed), try a 14g hoop. If a 14g hoop will not go in, use a 16g hoop, then after the piercing is healed you can go back to 14g jewelry. (The piercing will need to be tapered to insert the 14g jewelry.) Try not to irritate the piercing too much when reinserting the jewelry.

My piercing is red and swollen. What should I do? Some piercings may swell within the first few days and be tender and this is normal. If a new piercing is red and swollen, that does not necessarily mean it is infected. It is normal for a piercing that is healing to have a clear or milky discharge. However, if the discharge is green or yellow, it could be infected; only a doctor can tell you for sure. Most problems with piercings can be easily taken care of with proper cleaning or changing the jewelry to a different metal. If the piercing is so swollen that it is trying to swallow the jewelry, then a longer bar or hoop needs to be put in.

Sometimes a piercing can be red and irritated because of what the person is cleaning it with or he or she may be overcleaning the piercing. The first step would be to change what is being used to clean the piercing to something milder, and only clean it once or twice a day. Some people clean their new piercing several times a day causing extreme irritation. If they change how they are cleaning it and if after a few days the irritation has not gotten better, then they need to consider if they are having a reaction to the metal. Nickel allergies are seen occasionally, and removing the surgical steel and putting in titanium could solve the problem.

The only time jewelry should be changed in a new piercing is to relieve swelling or if there is a possibility of a metal allergy.

3. *I suspect my piercing is infected. What should I do?* First, anytime you touch the piercing, make sure your hands are clean. Check the area for a bubble or cyst. If your piercing is infected, leave your jewelry in so the infection can drain. We recommend cleaning the piercing once in the morning and once at night with the Sweet Pea Piercing Solution. Sometimes the piercing is irritated because the customer is having a reaction to the jewelry, and simply putting in a different metal solves the problem. A body piercer is not legally allowed to diagnose an infection, only a medical doctor can do that. Dr. Werschler of the Spokane Dermatology Clinic told me that if what is recommended by a professional piercer does not resolve the concern, he recommends using a topical antibiotic ointment for mild infections and an antibiotic for more serious ones.

4. *My piercing has a bubble. What do I do?* If the piercing develops a bubble or a cyst, it could be either infectious or noninfectious,

and draining the cyst can speed healing. Clean the area with the care solutions recommended above. When the cyst is drained, sometimes lightly colored ooze will come out and sometimes it will just bleed. Either way, it is good because it is draining. Watch the bubble, because when it is drained, it can fill up again right away and may need to be drained again. This can be repeated twice a day until the bubble dries up and goes away. If it is not allowed to drain, the bubble (cyst) can harden into a hypertrophic scar. The hypertrophic scar will never go away, so it is important to treat the cyst as soon as it shows up. Sometimes this happens because the body is having a reaction to the jewelry and simply changing from surgical steel to titanium can solve the problem. A piercing can also get a bubble on it if it gets pulled on or if a foreign substance gets into the piercing. It is important to leave the jewelry in so the piercing can drain. If the jewelry is removed, the piercing will heal shut, closing the infection inside the body. If you aren't able to resolve the issue, you should seek medical attention.

It's important to remember—and worth repeating—that there are several things that may cause irritation and possibly infect the piercing. These include touching the piercing with dirty hands, wearing dirty clothes over the piercing, sleeping on bedding that is not clean, tugging on the jewelry, having the piercing licked by pets, and not rinsing soap or shampoo completely away from the piercing.

5. *It looks as if the inside of my skin is coming out on the bottom of my navel piercing.* Occasionally someone will have a metal allergy and the body will try to reject the piercing. It looks like skin is coming out from the inside of the piercing. If surgical steel is in, try changing to titanium, and if titanium is in, try changing to surgical steel or gold. Bioflex and acrylic can also be tried. In most cases as soon as the metal irritation is removed, the piercing heals up nicely. There are the rare exceptions that no matter how hard someone tries, the body will not accept a certain piercing. You should keep in mind that when the body is pierced, a foreign object is being inserted into the body and it is the body's natural reaction to push the

foreign object out. The healthier the body is, the faster the piercing will heal.

6. *My new piercing is swollen; is there anything I can do about it?* Taking an anti-inflammatory such as Ibuprofen works well for swelling.[20] For oral (tongue and lip) piercings, in addition to taking an anti-inflammatory, ice placed on the piercing will help to reduce the swelling.

7. *My new piercing is bleeding; is that normal?* Sometimes for the first week or so, some piercings will bleed a little bit. If you have quite a bit of bleeding the first day, use cotton-tipped swabs and apply pressure to both sides of the piercing. Hold the pressure until the bleeding stops. For tongue piercings, hold pressure with cotton-tipped swabs, on the top and bottom, then apply ice on the tongue (don't chew it, just let it sit there). Rotate a few minutes of pressure and then a few minutes of ice, until the bleeding stops. If there is an unusual amount of bleeding, the customer should go back to their piercer to make sure a vein wasn't pierced and to see if the piercer recommends removing the jewelry.

   Tip: Caffeine, alcohol, aspirin, and some medications can thin the blood and can cause the new piercing to bleed more. By avoiding caffeine, alcohol, and aspirin, you reduce the chance of bleeding.

8. *I have a lump inside my new piercing; is there something wrong with it?* It is normal to feel a bump inside a new piercing. Fibroplasia is a normal healing response with scar tissue that may remain permanently or slowly be resolved by the body. In most cases, as the piercing heals on the inside the lump will go away.

9. *I want to get repierced but have scar tissue; can I get pierced in the same place?* It is not a good idea to pierce through scar tissue because scar tissue is not vascular (containing blood vessels) and is not conducive to healing.

---

20   www.drugs.com/ibuprofen.

10. *Why do piercings grow out?* Most piercings grow out because not enough skin was pierced. It is the body's natural reaction to try to reject the foreign object. It's harder for the body to reject a piercing that has an adequate amount of skin pierced. It is also important to pierce with the correct gauge to increase the chance the body will accept the piercing. It is easier for the body to reject thinner gauges, especially on the belly button and eyebrow. Although it is rare, there are occasions when the body will not accept a piercing.

11. *I've had a tummy tuck; can I get my belly button pierced?* The skin is so tight after a tummy tuck that it will not always hold the piercing, rejecting it the majority of the time. We recommend waiting awhile for the skin to relax and stretch out a bit before having it pierced. We ask women to wait a year after having this procedure before attempting to get pierced. There is no way to guarantee the piercing will hold.

12. *Does piercing hurt?* For most people, it is only a fast pinch, although some people do not even feel it. We offer topical anesthetic gel to numb the skin and a topical anesthetic spray to numb the tongue and inside of the lip. You can call piercing shops to see if you can find a body piercer who uses topical anesthetics. The majority of our customers are surprised by how quick the piercing is, and if they do feel anything, it only lasts for a second or two. As soon as the needle is pushed through, the pain, if any is felt, is relieved.

Most people only feel pressure for a couple of seconds. If the piercer is really fast, the customer should barely feel anything. Piercers who are new or not confident tend to pierce slower, which inflicts more pain on their customers. The other thing that can cause major discomfort to the person is if the piercer loses connection with the jewelry (this can happen during the initial piercing if the jewelry does not get inserted all the way through the piercing). We have had customers tell us that the clamp hurt more than the piercing. It is important to find a piercer who uses the freehand piercing technique.

13. *I have a bruise around my new piercing; was it done wrong?* We see bruising from time to time. If the skin bruises when it is pierced, it could be due to a vitamin deficiency. We have found that taking a multivitamin (a whole food supplement is even better), plus an extra vitamin C and zinc helps the bruising go away faster and will help the body heal faster. If the bruise is in the shape of the clamp, then that is how it was caused.

14. *Can I go swimming after I get pierced?* Yes, you just have to be careful. If you swim in a chlorinated pool or hot tub, you need to make sure the chlorine levels are where they should be so that there will be no bacteria in the water. Lakes, rivers, and oceans are fine to swim in as long as the water is clean. These are large bodies of water so you usually do not have to worry about picking up human bacteria. When you finish swimming, clean your new piercing with care solution.

15. *Can I take a bath with a new piercing?* When it comes to bathing, a shower is preferable to a bath, as bath water harbors bacteria. If you choose to take a bath, shower off afterward and gently wash your new piercing with a mild soap and rinse well.

16. *I'm going on vacation; is there anything I should worry about with my piercing?* Very often people go out of town and have problems with their new piercings. It could get irritated by any number of reasons, and you need to be prepared. I have talked to numerous people this has happened to and they lose their piercing because they were not prepared. It's a good idea to travel with care solution, an extra piece of jewelry, O-rings, and an extra bead.

I hate to admit this, but it did happen to me. I had a new labret piercing and we went to stay with some friends at their lake cabin. I had just changed to the shorter bar because my swelling was gone (I had been pierced for three weeks). I was talking and my labret bar caught on my teeth and pulled hard (this can happen if the 5/16″ bar is still too long). It started swelling and two days later, it was hurting pretty bad. I did not have my piercing bar with me to put in to make it more comfortable and I did not pack care solution. It hurt so bad that I had to take out the jewelry to relieve the pressure. After that incident, I never travel without backup jewelry and care solution. When you are traveling, it is possible to easily lose beads off your jewelry, so it is a good idea to take backup jewelry with you so if you do lose a bead, you will not lose the piercing.

I have also had an O-ring pulled off the back of my tunnel (stretched piercing on my ear) from a snorkel mask. I did not have an extra O-ring with me and the tunnel would not stay in without one, so I now also travel with an extra set of plugs or tunnels, just in case.

17. *Is it okay to pierce through veins?* No, absolutely not. With piercings in the ears and mouth, the piercer needs to carefully examine the area for veins. It is best to use a pen light or small flashlight to examine the area before piercing. A person may not be able to get a piercing due to where their veins are.

18. *Surface piercings look really cool and I'm thinking about getting one.* Think very carefully before getting a surface piercing. We will not do them at my stores because even though they look really cool, they grow out and leave a scar. Consider a dermal-anchor piercing instead of a surface piercing; it has a higher probability of staying in.

19. *I want to get a piercing but I need to hide it for work.* There are *retainers* made for all piercings. This is a translucent piece of jewelry that hides the piercing. Some piercings require metal jewelry to be worn until after the piercing is healed. After that, a retainer can be put in.

20. *Will my tongue be numb after I get it pierced?* On the rare occasion, someone will say that their tongue feels numb after he or she gets it pierced. This is not very common and is caused by the excessive swelling that comes with tongue piercing.

Once the swelling goes down, the tongue will feel normal again.

21. *I've had my navel pierced before but took the jewelry out. Can I have it pierced again?* We see girls who had a navel piercing and for various reasons (had a baby, got an infection, unsuccessfully pierced it themselves, or it grew out), they took out their jewelry. They come in wanting to be repierced but sometimes there is scar tissue in the area where the bar would sit straight up and down, so we pierce them at a slant to avoid the scar tissue. If there is no scar tissue from the previous piercing, it can be pierced in the same place, but if a lump of scar tissue can be seen or felt, it should not be pierced through because it may not heal properly.

22. *Can you pierce the sides of the tongue?* The tongue should only be pierced vertically, through the center. I will not pierce the sides of the tongue because it is too dangerous, and not many people's tongues qualify for this type of piercing anyway. It is not worth the risk of hitting one of the big veins that run through the tongue. The tongue should never be pierced horizontally. I had a customer who had his tongue pierced vertically on the side by someone else, and he asked if I performed this type of piercing. I explained to him why it is not safe. He said, "Yeah, the guy who pierced me had sweat running off his face while he was doing the piercing." And you let him go through with it?

23. *Can I go without wearing body jewelry in my piercing?* We recommend always wearing jewelry in your piercing. This way you are guaranteed your piercing will never heal up. With ear piercings, it is best to keep jewelry in for the first year. After that, it varies person to person who can go without jewelry and who cannot. Some people can go without wearing a bar in their tongue for weeks. For most people though, the piercing will heal shut, sometimes within the first day. For all piercings, the best rule is to leave the jewelry in. Many people lose their piercings because they have to take their jewelry out for surgery. I always recommend putting in retainers. Doctors will allow

acrylic retainers to be left in piercings for surgery, but they do not want metal jewelry in the body because it interferes with monitoring and electrosurgery equipment. A new exception to this is medical grade titanium microdermal anchors, as explained in another chapter. As medical procedures and equipment continue to change, what is allowed to be worn in the body during medical procedures could also change.

24. *Is it safe to get a piercing if you are pregnant?* There is no right or wrong answer to this question; it is best weighed by risk versus benefit. For earlobes, it is generally considered safe. For mucosal piercing (mucous membranes as such as in the nose and mouth), it isn't necessarily recommended. If the pregnant woman is healthy and not diabetic and not at high risk, it can be similar to other minor procedures such as injections or removal of moles.[21]

25. *Can I breast-feed if I have a nipple piercing?* As soon as a woman finds out she is pregnant she should remove the nipple jewelry to allow the piercing to heal closed. It does not harm the nipple to have a piercing, but when the milk comes through, if the piercing is not healed, it will squirt milk in three directions. This makes it harder, but not impossible for the baby to nurse. This information should be told to all young women before they get their nipples pierced. Even if there is scar tissue in the nipple, the milk will find a way to get through. Although it is completely safe and will not hinder breast-feeding, the nipple piercing is best done after the woman is finished having babies.

An article from the LaLeche League warns that choking is a potential hazard for the baby if the mother does not remove the jewelry prior to breast-feeding. During breast-feeding beads could come off and jewelry could come out of the piercing and lodge in the baby's throat. It is also possible for the baby's gums, tongue, and the soft and hard palate to be injured while sucking on the jewelry. It was also noted that women who did not remove their jewelry prior to nursing encountered

---

21   Werschler, Personal Interview.

difficulties including poor latch, gagging, slurping, and milk leaking from the baby's mouth.[22]

26. *Do I have to take my navel jewelry out if I get pregnant?* I have seen some women save their navel piercing during their pregnancy by being very careful to keep jewelry in that is long enough to allow the skin to stretch. It is possible to get very long navel Bioflex bars for this purpose. I have also heard of women putting nylon line (like a heavy fishing line) in their piercing to keep it open, and then they have it stretched back out with a taper after they have the baby.

Advanced Registered Nurse Practitioner Karen Kuehn told me that when she sees girls who have had their navels pierced before they got pregnant, after they had their baby, some of them had stretch marks that spider up the stomach from where the navel was pierced. This is unusual, as she has not seen this on girls who did not have their navels pierced before their pregnancy.[23]

27. *Are there any circumstances under which I should not get a piercing?* If you have rheumatic heart disease, heart murmur, diabetes, bleeding diathesis (susceptibility to bleeding/hemorrhage), AIDS, are subject to fainting, or are taking any medications that thin your blood, and you are concerned about getting a piercing, you should seek the advice of your physician before getting pierced. Having these conditions does not mean you should not get pierced, but if you have any concerns, discuss it with your doctor first. Those with diabetes may find that it takes longer for their piercing to heal. My daughter has diabetes and has never had any problems with her piercings healing in the proper amount of time, but every person is different.

28. *Are there any metals I should not wear in my piercings?* Use common sense when wearing any kind of jewelry. We see

---

22   La Leche League, www.llli.org.

23   Karen Kuehn, MSN, ARNP, Personal Interview, 17 Mar. 2008, Valley Obstetrics & Gynecology PS, Spokane Valley, WA.

people with paperclips, nails, and safety pins among other things in their piercings. Your body can have an unwanted reaction to these types of materials because they are not made to wear in piercings. For body piercings, only quality body jewelry should be worn.

For ear piercings there are earrings made from many different materials and you need to be cautious about what you put in your ears. Earrings that are silver-plated or gold-plated frequently cause extreme irritation to the piercing. This type of jewelry can make the piercing red and very sore.

Sterling silver jewelry is very good quality but should only be worn in healed ear or nose piercings. If you wear sterling silver jewelry, keep an eye on it because it could cause a complication to your piercing. The sterling silver reacts to acids in the body, which makes the metal tarnish. If this happens, the piercing can absorb the tarnish, and a dark discoloration appears at the piercing site that will never go away. The more acid in your system, the higher the chance of making the metal tarnish. There are some factors that can create more acid in the body; these are stress, drinking acidic fruit juices, and taking aspirin.

While most people can wear sterling silver earrings, some are allergic to them because sterling silver has nickel in it. There are manufacturers who make sterling silver earrings without nickel, and their earrings are great.

29. *Is there any part of the body I should not get pierced?* There are body piercers out there who will pierce any part of the body. Just because a piercer is willing to pierce any area of the body does not mean it is right or that you should do it.

30. *There is a lot of conflicting information on the Internet; can I trust what I read?* I am so tired of all the articles written on the Internet against body piercing. I am tired of ordinary citizens posting incorrect information on websites about body piercing. One such person suggests doing research about body

piercing before having it done and then goes on to provide incorrect information about piercing. Maybe she should have done some research before writing the article. Her point was to advise teenagers against body piercing by writing misleading information. Using such scare tactics does not deter the average teenager from getting pierced. People look to the Internet for information, but there is no easy way to know if what you are reading is coming from a reputable source.

I love using the Internet and it is a great source to research many different subjects. When it comes to body piercing that will be performed on your own body, it is better to research this with body piercers face-to-face.

31. *I have heard of self-piercing kits; are they safe?* I have nothing good to say about self-piercing kits. I am horrified that these kits are being placed into the hands of the public. I was at a trade show where someone was selling self-piercing kits. These piercing kits contain a needle, a piece of jewelry, and a clamp. Upon closer inspection of these self-piercing kits, I found that most of them did not have the correct size or type of jewelry needed for the intended piercing. I had to purchase one because it was so unbelievable. The tongue kit that I purchased came with a 14g 5/8″ tongue bar (which is the wrong length, too short for piercing) and the tongue bar had acrylic beads on it (which you should never pierce with). The package claimed to be sterile, but the jewelry was in a ziplock bag with a staple through it. The jewelry was then placed into plastic packaging along with the sterile needle and clamp. The entire package was hole-punched (to hang on a display) allowing air in. If the package was sterile to begin with, as it claimed, the sterilization was compromised when it was hole punched and stapled. The other thing that was weird about the packaging was how many words were misspelled, including tongue. The piercing instructions that were included did not give enough information for someone to properly perform a body piercing. My staff and I played with the clamp that was enclosed and we could not get it to work properly.

The danger of self-piercing kits is that in a home-piercing situation, a needle could be shared by more than one person, spreading disease. There is also the danger of piercing through veins or other areas that are not meant to be pierced. A higher risk of infection is likely to occur from using tools and jewelry that are not properly sterilized.

32. *What should I do if I get a piercing but I am not happy with it?* Certainly every piercer should strive to do a perfect piercing, every time, every day of the week. The reality is that, once in a while, a piercing does not come out the way the piercer anticipated. At my stores, this is a very rare occurrence, but because we are human, unfortunately, it can happen. I train my piercers to be in the moment, not distracted and not thinking of other things when they are piercing someone. If a piercing comes out crooked or if the placement is off, the piercer should acknowledge what happened and repierce immediately. If the customer gets home and takes a good look at the piercing and realizes it is not placed where it should be, he or she should return to the piercing shop where he or she was pierced, at their earliest convenience (don't put this off), to discuss with the piercer what their options are. Always leave the jewelry in, so the piercer can see how the jewelry sits and if it was done correctly.

33. *Can I donate blood after I get a piercing?* Generally, blood banks will not let anyone donate blood for one year after getting a piercing, but there are exceptions. In our community, our local blood bank has approved our piercing method and will allow our customers to donate blood after receiving a piercing as long as we provide proper paperwork to the blood bank. Check with your local blood bank to see what their policy is.

CHAPTER TWENTY-FIVE

Ear-Piercing Guns

I t is widely rumored among body piercers that piercing guns should not be used for cartilage piercing because it breaks the cartilage. In the last twelve years, we have done over twenty-five thousand ear piercings with piercing guns and have never seen or heard of an actual case where this happened. (See box below for information on a study regarding this.)

There is absolutely nothing wrong with using piercing guns to pierce earlobes and cartilage, as long as it is the type of piercing system that uses piercing studs that are *completely encapsulated.* There is currently only one brand available in the United States that I will use, the Studex System 75, and I have used this piercing system for lobe and cartilage piercings since 1998.

With the Studex ear-piercing system that I use, the studs are completely encapsulated and sterile. The entire capsule (cartridge) containing one single-piercing stud is loaded onto the piercing instrument (gun) while it is still inside its sterile package. After the piercing is performed, the entire capsule is disposed of. With this type of system, there is no risk of cross-contamination of any type of bacteria or blood-borne pathogen from one customer to another. Everything that touches the person's ear is discarded. Because a single stud is secured in the capsule, the gun can be tilted sideways and even turned upside down to better position the stud on the ear. With this system, the piercing can also be done using only the cartridge; without loading it into the gun/piercing instrument, ensuring everything used for the piercing is disposable.

The Studex system is a hand-force system, which means the piercer uses hand pressure to pierce the stud through the ear. This ensures that the piercing stud successfully goes through the ear every time. The piercing studs available with this system are made from medical-grade surgical steel, titanium, hermetical gold, and 14 kt gold.

One issue, which could possibly develop from piercing an earlobe with a gun, is that the stud may not be long enough to allow for excessive swelling. We examine each person's lobe to see how thick it is, and if the customer's lobe is fairly thick, we offer a longer piercing stud or we offer a body piercing with a hoop. If a thick lobe is pierced with a standard-length piercing stud and it has excessive swelling, the lobe could swallow the piercing stud. For any piercing done with a piercing gun or a needle, it is the responsibility of the piercer to examine the area of the piercing in order to choose the correct jewelry. Simply piercing with the correct jewelry to begin with will eliminate this complication. Not all piercing-stud systems offer a long post for piercing.

Another ear-piercing system I have used is the Blomdahl system, which is now being marketed only to physicians. It is a wonderful ear-piercing system that has been examined by OSHA (Occupational Safety and Health Administration) and has met all of OSHA's blood-borne pathogens compliance standards. This spring-loaded piercing gun uses an encapsulated, sterile cartridge containing the piercing stud, and is disposed of after the piercing. This piercing gun is from Sweden, and anyone interested in finding a doctor using this system, should contact Blomdahl for a referral to a physician in their area.

Not all piercing guns are alike. Spring-loaded piercing guns requiring manual insertion of the piercing stud are another type of piercing gun, and they give all piercing guns a bad name. With this type of system, the piercing studs are loaded into the gun by hand. When the piercing is performed, the ear touches the piercing gun where the studs sit, so everyone's ear touches the same part of the gun during the piercing. Occasionally these guns will not shoot the stud all the way through the ear, so the piercer has to remove the stud and repierce. When the stud is pulled out, it causes the ear to bleed. There is no way to sterilize these guns in between each piercing, making it possible to spread blood-borne pathogens. Be aware that there are still businesses that use this type of gun.

With regard to aftercare for ears pierced with studs, the person needs to clean the piercing twice a day with care solution, making sure to clean between the jewelry and the front of the ear and between the back of the ear and the clasp. When it is time to change the earrings (six weeks), we recommend the customer return to us to help remove the back of the piercing stud. These studs have locking backs, and we can easily remove the back with our ring-opener tool.

While most body piercers frown on piercing ears with piercing guns, it is important to remember that complications can arise from any piercing, whether it was performed with a piercing gun or a needle. This is where it is crucial to use common sense. Some body piercers say that ear-piercing guns are bad because they break cartilage and produce micro spray (microscopic sprays of blood). Neither of these two rumors can be validated.

When I was attending committee meetings in Olympia, Washington, for the formation of state body-piercing regulations, I presented the committee with a Studex System 75 ear-piercing cartridge and demonstrated how to use it. I was surprised to discover that the piercers in attendance, who were pushing to have the law changed to eliminate cartilage piercings with guns, had never seen a gun-piercing system or seen how it worked. I have found this to be consistent with other body piercers I have met who want to dismiss the use of piercing guns. Despite being presented with this ear-piercing system and sharing in my personal experiences, the committee in no way deterred their outlook on piercing guns. From the discussion that ensued, it made me wonder if, in part, they condemned the use of piercing guns in order to bring more ear-piercing business to their shops and to take business away from retailers doing ear piercing with guns in shopping malls.

Below is information about a study performed in 2006 that compares gun piercings to needle piercings.

Do Piercing Guns Break the Cartilage?

Purpose of the study: To evaluate the extent of damage to ear cartilage using different piercing techniques.

Methods: Twenty-two fresh human-cadaver ears were pierced using two spring-loaded piercing guns (Caflon and Blomdahl), one hand-force system (Studex), and a piercing needle (16G i.v. catheter).

In the 2006 study, twenty-two ears were pierced using the following methods:
22 needle piercings
22 hand-force piercings (Studex system)
22 spring-loaded piercing gun piercings (Caflon system)
20 spring-loaded piercings (Blomdahl system)

The study was done to see if piercing guns caused more damage to the cartilage than a piercing needle did. The study proved that, "A comparison between the different piercing methods *did not show any significant difference* in perichondrial damage, total chondral tears, or chondral shattering, despite the fact that the design and diameter of the tip of the piercing instrument varied greatly, as well as the force applied to pierce the ear."

"In conclusion, what this study does show is that the currently available methods to pierce the upper ear are comparable with regard to direct tissue damage."[24]

The only valid reason I would ever give for having a cartilage piercing done with a hoop (needle piercing) rather than stud (gun piercing), is for comfort or aesthetics. When the cartilage is healing and still tender, it is much more comfortable to sleep on a hoop than it is with a stud. The benefit of having a hoop in a new piercing is that it allows more airflow through the piercing to initiate healing; however, we have not seen a noticeable difference in healing between the two types of piercings.

---

24   Van Wijk, M P, et al., "Ear piercing techniques and their effect on cartilage, a histologic study," *J Plast Reconstr Aesthet Surg* (2007): doi:1016/j.bjps.2007.01.077.

CHAPTER TWENTY-SIX

Piercing the Ears of Children

We are frequently asked to pierce the ears of babies and toddlers. For several years we did pierce children, six months and older, with piercing guns. Piercing a child who does not understand what is being done to them raises all kinds of issues.

Some children are able to sit still for several minutes while they are being pierced, but many children cannot. What we often encountered was a female child who wanted to get her ears pierced while at home, but as soon as she sat in our chair, she became scared that it was going to hurt, and the struggle to pierce her would begin. We always felt bad for the child, but the mother would want her daughter's ears pierced so bad that we would keep trying. There were many times that we would not be able to pierce a child due to the struggle to get to her ears. The shoulder would come up, covering the earlobe. There were also times that the child would physically struggle with us. The last time I got kicked in the stomach while trying to pierce a toddler's ears was the day I quit piercing children. That day we changed our policy to only pierce children six years and older. We will make an exception if a child can come in and tell us that she or he wants the piercing, or if the child will sit still without squirming. We refer all others to the stores in our mall that pierce children.

One thing to be aware of when piercing babies is that even if the earrings are placed perfectly centered in the lobe, when that little girl grows up and her ears develop, the ears will not grow the same. No one has perfectly matching ears; the left ear is always different from the right. When the ears develop, one hole may be higher or lower than the other, or the piercing may be off center. I've always explained this to parents so they will not be surprised if it should happen to their daughter.

The Studex ear-piercing system has shorter piercing studs for babies and small children, which are a better fit in the earlobe than the average-length piercing stud.

After the six-week healing period, good quality earrings should always be worn. This is very important during the first year and always while the ears are healing in order to avoid problems with metal allergies.

CHAPTER TWENTY-SEVEN

A Message from the Body Piercers

From where we stand as body piercers, watching our customers walk through the door, we enjoy the experience from beginning to end. It is our job to educate and help our customers through the process.

Please feel free to ask us questions, because we want you to enjoy your piercing experience as much as we do.

I asked the body piercers who work for me and a friend who bought one of my stores to add their thoughts about body piercing to this book. This is what they have to say:

> Most people don't know that piercing can be done without using clamps; they have not heard of the freehand piercing, and they are surprised that we do it this way.
>
> *Jacqueline Schwartz, body piercer*
> *Silver Safari, Bellingham, Washington*

The best part about being a body piercer is the satisfaction of giving the customer not only a beautiful piercing but a fantastic piercing experience as well. Getting any piercing is nerve-racking, no matter who you are, and the atmosphere and piercer's attitude can greatly affect the customer one way or another.

I like to treat my customers how I would want to be treated when faced with something exciting yet a little scary! Putting a smile on my face, having a calm demeanor, and being 100 percent invested in their experience is key for me every time.

When customers are happy and composed, they will remember their piercing positively. They will have a little more knowledge about piercing and make the world of body modification a little less daunting.

I love my job and the piercings I get to do. Working for Genia is a wonderful learning opportunity and an adventure every day. I wouldn't trade it for anything.

Georgie Young, body piercer
Silver Safari, Spokane, Washington

I was destined for the world of body piercing. When I was sixteen, I made jewelry and sold it to a local piercing shop; when they offered me a job, I was super excited until my dad put a halt to that dream. I always had it in the back of my mind that it would be the coolest job ever. January 5, 2004, at the age of twenty-four, I saw the start of having the coolest job ever and my dreams coming true. Life at Silver Safari is educational, entertaining, and all about having great experiences.

My training started with learning the different gauges, lengths, and types of body jewelry. I also learned the different body piercings you can put different jewelry in; for example, you can put a nose stud in a fossa or put a labret bar in a tragus. I was trained to pierce ears with piercing guns and change body jewelry. Learning went pretty smoothly and I enjoyed working in this environment.

Then a body-piercing position opened up, and I got the job. Genia herself trained me on all the different piercings and techniques. I have to say "Genia herself," because now I do all the training. In our shop, she's a legend.

I have discovered I can joke with the customers to get them to relax a little during the process. We have a good laugh, and a good laugh seems to relax people; then I can go on to answer questions and put them at ease. I love customer service. I like helping our customers with jewelry choices, piercing choices, and helping them with whatever it is I can, while providing them with information to help them with their piercing.

What I love about Silver Safari is the atmosphere, jewelry selection, and the way we manage the store. Our care instructions are very easy to learn, and we give care solution out with every piercing.

We're educating ourselves all the time and helping others to be educated. My husband can tell when I'm getting ready for work rather than any other day, because I'm doing the happy dance. I love going to work, and I love my job. I was destined to work at Silver Safari; this shop is clean, comfortable, and just my kind of atmosphere.

Rebecca Lopez, manager and body piercer
Silver Safari, NorthTown Mall, Spokane, Washington

When I first began working at Silver Safari, Genia had been the only piercer in the store for a year and a half. It was shortly after I was hired that she started training some of the sales staff to be body piercers. I had been hired to sell jewelry, pierce ears, and change jewelry, but little did I know that I had so much to learn. I was apprehensive in the beginning, and for weeks I would try to watch an entire experience of someone getting a piercing done—including the needle piercing through skin, whether it be an ear, a lip, or, the worst for me to watch at that time, a tongue. Through the years and from the many customers that walked into that shop, I gained confidence and actually started enjoying watching the entire procedure, from the time customers walked in proclaiming their desire for a new body accessory, to the time they walked out. I developed an interest to do the procedures myself. They fascinated me.

I was trained to pierce at the Spokane store, and then I had a short stint managing and piercing at Silver Safari in Las Vegas before we moved that store to Bellingham, Washington, where I took on full-time management of the Bellingham store.

Becoming a body piercer was something I never saw myself doing as a career before getting a job at Silver Safari. However, it is one of the greatest things I have ever come upon. I meet new, interesting people every day, not to mention all the customers who come back to me, remembering that I pierced them in the past and appreciating the work that I did. Body piercing is different from any other type of job; you are modifying someone's body in a very physical way, hoping that every piercing you do is exactly what they imagined. There is a lot of pressure that comes along with the job. Your credibility depends on every move that you make, and there is a lot of pressure associated with that. You hope that everything you do day after day will make an impression on that person in a very positive way. They walk away from you with something that they could have for years.

Over the years—which, by the way, I have been a certified body piercer since 2005 (and have worked at Silver Safari since 2002)—I have learned and perfected every technique for every piercing I have been trained to do.

Piercing is a job you learn from experience. Which definitely defines practice makes perfect, or as Genia would say, "Perfect practice makes perfect." You could be a piercer for twenty-plus years and still be learning. Our focus is for every piercing to come out right and I think every piercer understands this, because the piercer must ensure that the piercing comes out right every time, with little or no room for error. All in all, when you love what you do, and you make the best of what you do, you will love your job. People will love and be satisfied with the job you do, and for me that is very satisfying. They come back to me and remember my name, even though sometimes all I can remember is their hair, their smile, or the septum ring I put in their nose the other day.

Joanna Schlosser, manager and body piercer
Silver Safari, Bellingham, Washington

Working at Silver Safari has been such a tremendous experience. I never thought I would be a body piercer, but I am so glad that I was offered the job and took it. I love what I do! I enjoy being able to provide a service to the customer and not only give her or him what he or she wants but go above and beyond their expectations. From the time he or she walks into the store to the time he or she leaves with the piercing and care solution, I take the opportunity to get to know the person, to understand how he or she is feeling, and to learn how I can help them relax so that their time and money are well spent. I make sure they are 100 percent satisfied. Body modification is not cheap, and you get what you pay for, which some people don't realize. After working at Silver Safari, I wouldn't go anywhere else to get pierced. I know what I'm getting, and I know that we are a clean shop that is up to code and licensed through Washington State. We have been trained by the best, and we are the best. I really don't think a lot of other piercing shops can compare!

My recommendation to someone wanting to get pierced is to make sure you go in before you get the piercing and get a feel for the shop; make sure you're comfortable, and don't be afraid to ask questions about the process. Or just come in and see us and experience it for yourself!

Jordan Hemmert, body piercer
Silver Safari, Spokane, Washington

One thing we see often in this industry is shops offering deeply discounted specials on piercings. While this doesn't always guarantee there will be issues, there is usually a reason that certain businesses need to offer services at such a cheap rate. Those reasons generally have to do with a piercer's inexperience, a shop that is not getting enough business, or a piercer who is willing to cut corners to make the procedure inexpensive. Any of these reasons should make you question whether you should get a piercing at that shop. Look for places that have a reputation for being clean and thorough, and are staffed with well-trained, licensed, and experienced piercers. Don't be afraid to ask the right questions before getting pierced! We often have to fix piercings done by discount shops by replacing inappropriate jewelry with correct jewelry or by redoing the piercing altogether if placement is incorrect. Sometimes these cheap piercings end up costing people more money than if they would have spent the money upfront to do it correctly the first time. Do your homework and save yourself trouble (and possibly extra money) in the long run.

Something else to keep in mind is that all body piercings need time to heal properly. Be patient and give your piercing the appropriate amount of time before you start changing the jewelry. This amount of time is different for most piercings, but your piercer should verbally tell you when you can change your jewelry, and it should be written on the aftercare sheet he or she sends home with you. Just because you can start changing the jewelry, does not mean that the piercing is completely healed yet. For some people, piercings can take up to a year to completely heal (there is an exception for oral piercings, which tend to heal much faster). During that first year, piercings are still susceptible to problems like swelling, infections, heightened metal sensitivities, and rejections. To help reduce these types of issues, it's best not to change it too often during that first year and only purchase high-quality metals or medical-grade plastics. If you are not sure, visit a reputable store that can help you select appropriate jewelry and can assist you in changing it if needed. Again, following certain protocol in the beginning and not necessarily going the cheap and seemingly easy route will likely save you time, money, and hassle in the long run. And your piercing will thank you for it!

Jacqueline Gibson, owner and body piercer
Silver Safari, Spokane Valley, Washington

Chapter Twenty-Eight

Piercing Stories

When I started researching where I was going to open my second store, my husband called all of the competitors in the cities we were considering. When he called each piercing shop, he said he wanted to bring in his thirteen-year-old daughter to have her belly button pierced and wanted information about price and what was included with the piercing. One piercer told him he had one set price for all piercings above the waist and one set price for all piercings below the waist. The body piercer explained, if the nipples hung below the waist, the piercing would be the higher price. Evidently, this piercer thought he was quite the comedian but somewhere in the conversation lost sight of the fact that he was talking to a dad who was inquiring about a belly piercing for his young daughter. Another piercer told my husband, "If we can grab it, we can stab it." Doesn't really make you want to rush your thirteen-year-old in for a piercing, does it?

* * * * *

When I first started piercing, I had a mom bring in her thirteen-year-old daughter to have her belly button pierced. When this girl was born, she was born with her stomach on the outside of her body. She had surgery to have her stomach put back inside and the doctor created a belly button for her, which had to be put on the side of her stomach. This is my all-time favorite piercing. This girl was so proud to have her belly button pierced, and I am honored that I got to do that for her.

* * * * *

I was walking through the mall and saw someone getting his ears pierced at a kiosk in the center of the mall. The person working at the kiosk loaded the studs into his spring-loaded piercing gun and pierced the customer's ear. That was it. He did not clean or mark the area he pierced, and he was not wearing gloves.

* * * * *

A few years ago, I kept waking up with an earache in my left ear. I made an appointment with a doctor to find out what was wrong. He took out his scope to look into my ear canal and before he even looked inside my ear he said, "Well, there's the problem right there" referring to my conch piercing. It took everything I had not to get sarcastic with him, but I assured him that I had been having the earaches before and after I had my conch pierced, so I was quite sure that was not what was causing it. As it turns out, the earache was caused from clenching my teeth when I sleep, which my dentist has helped me with by making me a bite guard.

* * * * *

My dentist has never scolded me for having my tongue and lip pierced, but I am careful to keep jewelry in my piercings that does not damage my teeth or gums. I sat next to a dentist on an airplane once and after we talked for a while about what he did, I knew the question was coming about what I did. He was not quite as friendly to me after I said the words "body piercer," and he made it very clear how he felt about chipped teeth caused from tongue piercings. I cannot disagree with the viewpoint of dentists on this subject. Many people wear jewelry that damages their teeth and gums.

This gave me the idea to create a brochure for dentists explaining the different lengths and types of jewelry worn in tongue piercings and how chipped teeth can be prevented. It is my hope that by educating the dentists on what jewelry should be worn in the mouth, they can help their patients to wear the correct jewelry—perhaps giving the dentist a more positive outlook on body piercing.

* * * * *

I do not like it when I hear negative stories from women who have had their nipples pierced by male piercers. One girl told me she was in the piercing room with her top off as requested by the piercer. Before piercing her, he made an excuse to leave the room. After he left, all the guys who were working at the shop walked through the room one at a time as she sat there with her top off. I have also had women tell me that the male piercers who pierced them made comments about their breasts while they were being pierced. One of my customers had gone to a piercing shop to see what it would cost to have her nipples pierced. The piercer told her he would do it for free if she would have lunch with him. I know not all male piercers are like this, but before getting a nipple piercing, make sure you are comfortable with the piercer.

* * * * *

We often have mothers bring in their teenage daughters for a belly-button or nose piercing. The mom gets so excited about it that after her daughter has been pierced, the mom decides to get pierced too. We perform lots of mother/daughter piercings and we love these. These piercings actually gave us the inspiration for one of our radio commercials. In the commercial, the dad acts totally surprised to find out his daughter has just gotten a navel piercing and he questions her about it. He is first surprised about the piercing, then is again surprised to find out it was done at the mall. He says to his wife, "You let her get that?" and the wife says, "Yeah, how do you like mine?"

* * * * *

CHAPTER TWENTY-NINE

Conclusion

When I was sixteen years old, I asked my mom if I could get the second holes in my ears pierced, and she said to ask my dad. Dad said no, I could not get my second holes pierced, but I could have a ring put in my nose if I wanted. He thought that was funny; back then the only ones with rings in their noses were bulls. Of course, this was in the 1970s, before we had heard of body piercing. Looking back now, I think it's funny that my dad made that statement.

I mentioned before that occasionally I take my mom to work with me. Since my daughter was three years old, she has been coming to work with me too, and she has grown up in my stores. By the time she was nineteen, she had a lot of piercings, but the only facial piercing she had was her nose. I would not let her pierce her eyebrow, lip, or tongue. I may be a body piercer, but I am still her mom. I believed she needed to keep her piercings in perspective, and she did not need to have everything pierced—even though while she was growing up she disagreed with me on this subject. I am still amused that when she turned eighteen, she asked my permission to get her tongue pierced. When she started working in my stores, I let her pierce my cartilage—yes, with a piercing gun! I am very proud that when she turned nineteen, she apprenticed to become one of my body piercers.

I have a great deal of respect for the human body, and I do not believe that it should necessarily be loaded up with steel, even though many people are doing that. I look at everything long-term. It is really fun and exciting to get piercings and stretch your ears when you are young, but how is it going to look when you get older? We need to make mature decisions about our bodies. I personally have a lot of piercings (seventeen) and two dermal anchors; with the exception of my second holes, which are stretched to a 6g, I wear very conservative jewelry. I live in two worlds, the world of body piercing and the world where people are not all pierced up, and I go back and forth between the two very comfortably.

For my mother's seventy-ninth birthday, she wanted her conch pierced. How cool is that? She also let me pierce her second holes, but so far has not let me pierce anything else on her. I keep trying to talk her into a nose piercing so that we will have three generations of nose piercings in our family. So far, she is not going for it. I do not push piercing on people who do not want it. It is my thing, and I respect those who do not care for it.

My husband does not have any piercings and although I am hopeful that one day he will let me pierce him, I respect his decision to keep his body the way it is. He respects the fact that I love all of my piercings, and he loves them too. He was not fazed on either of the two occasions that I came home with surprise labret piercings. He enjoys my world, and I enjoy his. When I follow him around at golf tournaments, you can be sure I am the only one on the golf course with facial piercings (especially at the country-club courses), and I enjoy that. I do not look like a body piercer, and it's fun to watch people's expression when they hear what I do. I never get tired of the shock value that being a body piercer holds. My husband, with his conservative golf background, spends a lot of time with me at my stores, and my customers talk quite openly to him about their piercings. When he first started spending time at my stores, a girl came in to the store and went into great detail to my husband about her piercing below the waist and the jewelry she had in and why her current jewelry was not working out. I wish I could have been there to see his face.

People are very open with their piercings, and even though we are body piercers, we are also a retail store in the mall. Even after all these years, we are still amused every time a woman comes in and lifts up her shirt to reveal her piercing and says, "I need one of these," instead of simply asking to see nipple jewelry.

I love body piercing. My piercings do not define who I am, but they definitely make my life more interesting. My knowledge and experience with piercing define who I am. I feel extremely lucky to own my own body-piercing business. This is the greatest job, and I have a great time doing it.

We are all given opportunities during our lifetime, and I am so grateful that this opportunity was presented to me. Everything happens for a reason—pay attention to your life so if an opportunity presents itself, you will reach out and grab it too!

Autoclave

A pressurized, steam-heated unit that is used to sterilize needles and tools used in piercing. It is much like a pressure cooker. The autoclave is heated to a degree that kills all Blood-Borne Pathogens and bacteria on tools. A spore test should be done on an autoclave and sent to an independent laboratory for testing; some states require monthly testing, and some require annual testing. This ensures that the autoclave is heating to the level required to sterilize. The laboratory test results (issued as a certificate) should be posted in the body-piercing studio.

Blood-borne pathogens

Causative agents of disease that can be found in the blood of an infected person. Body piercers are at risk of being exposed to blood-borne pathogens including hepatitis B (HBV), hepatitis C virus (HCV), and human immunodeficiency virus (HIV). Exposure can occur through needle sticks contaminated with an infected customer's blood.

Captive Hoop

A hoop that uses a bead to keep the hoop closed. Captive hoops are worn in many body piercings, such as ears, nose, and nipple. It is also called a captive-bead ring.

Diameter

The size across the circle of a captive hoop, measured from the inside (side to side) of the hoop.

Ear Piercings
- Anti-Tragus
- Cartilage
- Conch
- Daith
- Fossa

- Industrial
- Lobe
- Rook
- Tragus

FREEHAND PIERCING
A style of body piercing that is done using a needle and cork for the piercing, without the use of a clamp.

GAUGE
A measurement of the thickness of the body jewelry, whether it is a hoop or a bar. In this book, I abbreviate the word gauge by using a *g*. For example, 16g means sixteen gauge. The larger the gauge, the smaller (thinner) the jewelry will be. A 16g piece of jewelry is thin, while a 2g piece of jewelry is much thicker. In the measurement 14g 7/16˝, 14g is the thickness of the hoop or bar, and 7/16″ is its length (barbell) or diameter (hoop) in inches. Generally, the gauge on body jewelry is written as 16g, 16G, or 16ga.

LENGTH
Measurement of the longest dimension of a straight or curved barbell. Note that only the bar is measured (from end to end); the beads are not measured.

LIP PIERCINGS
- labret or lip (in the center or to the side, below the bottom lip)
- Marilyn Monroe (above the lip, to the side)
- Medusa (above the lip, centered in the dip)

RETAINER
A clear piece of body jewelry (acrylic or polycarbonate) that is worn to hide a piercing.

RING CLOSER
A tool used to close captive hoops.

RING OPENER
Also known as a ring expander, it is a tool used to open captive hoops and to set the bead into the captive hoop.

TAPER

A tool used to stretch/taper/gauge ears to a larger size. It looks like a needle but is not sharp on the end.

TAPERED OR GAUGED EARS

Ears that are stretched to wear larger jewelry.

"Body piercing: Piercing sites." *Women's Health Queensland Wide Inc.* (Sept. 17, 2008): http://www.womhealth.org.au.

"Frequently Asked Questions." The Association of Professional Piercers (Sept. 14, 2008): http://safepiercing.org.

"Hypertrophic Scars." A Board Certified Plastic Surgeon (Sept. 25, 2012): http://www.aboardcertifiedplasticsurgeonresource.com/scar-revision/hypertrophic-scars.html.

Kuehn, Karen, MSN, ARNP, Valley Obstetrics & Gynecology PS, Spokane Valley, WA. http://www.valobgyn.com.

Martin, Jahaan. "Nipple Piercing: Is It Compatible with Breast-Feeding?" *La Leche League International* (Sept. 17, 2008): http://www.llli.org/llleaderweb/LV/LVJunJul99p64.html.

Metzer, Donna I., MD. "Body Piercing: What You Should Know." *American Family Physician* (Sept. 25, 2012): http://www.aafp.org/afp/2005/1115/p2035.html.

Metzer, Donna I., MD. "Complications of Body Piercing." *American Family Physician* (Sept. 17, 2008): http://www.aafp.org/afp/2005/1115/p2029.html.

"Piercings: Proper care can help prevent complications" (Sept. 22, 2008): http://www.mayoclinic.com/health/piercings/SN00049.

Sappo Hill Soap. http://www.sappohill.com.

"Tattoos and Body Piercings for Minors." National Conference of Legislatures. *The Forum for America's Ideas* (Sept. 14, 2008): http://www.ncsl.org/programs/halth/minorbodyart.htm.

"Teflon." (Dec. 2, 2008): http://www.tuberose.com//Teflon.html.

"Titanium: The Medical Metal of Choice." (Sept. 8, 2011): http://www.supraalloys.com/medical-titanium.php.

Van Wijk, M P, et al. "Ear piercing techniques and their effect on cartilage, a histologic study." *Journal of Plastic Reconstructive & Aesthetic Surgery* (2007): dol:1016/j.bjps.2007.01.077.

"What Teflon Is And Why You Should Avoid It." *The Good Human* (Dec. 2, 2008): http://www.thegoodhuman.com/2007/07/31/what-teflon-is-and-why-you-should-avoid-it.

Werschler, Wm. Phillip, MD/FAAD/FAACS, Assistant Clinical Professor of Medicine/Dermatology, University of Washington, Seattle and Spokane Dermatology Clinic, Spokane, WA. www.spokanederm.com, WerschlerAesthetics.com.

Young, Cathy, DNSc, APRN, BC, and Myrna L. Armstrong, EdD, RN, FAAN. "What Nurses Need to Know When Caring for Women with Genital Piercings." *Nursing for Women's Health* (April/May 2008): 129–37.

Contact Information

If you would like to learn more about my stores, meet my staff, or contact me, please visit my website at silver-safari.com.